SYNCHRONIZING E-SECURITY

Advances in Information Security

Sushil Jajodia

Consulting editor
Center for Secure Information Systems
George Mason University
Fairfax, VA 22030-4444
email: jajodia@gmu.edu

The goals of Kluwer International Series on ADVANCES IN INFORMATION SECURITY are, one, to establish the state of the art of, and set the course for future research in information security and, two, to serve as a central reference source for advanced and timely topics in information security research and development. The scope of this series includes all aspects of computer and network security and related areas such as fault tolerance and software assurance.

ADVANCES IN INFORMATION SECURITY aims to publish thorough and cohesive overviews of specific topics in information security, as well as works that are larger in scope or that contain more detailed background information than can be accommodated in shorter survey articles. The series also serves as a forum for topics that may not have reached a level of maturity to warrant a comprehensive textbook treatment.

Researchers as well as developers are encouraged to contact Professor Sushil Jajodia with ideas for books under this series.

Additional titles in the series:

Additional information about this series can be obtained from
http://www.wkap.nl/prod/s/ADIS

SYNCHRONIZING E-SECURITY

by

Godfried Williams
Senior Lecturer
University of East London, United Kingdom

KLUWER ACADEMIC PUBLISHERS
Boston / Dordrecht / London

Distributors for North, Central and South America:
Kluwer Academic Publishers
101 Philip Drive
Assinippi Park
Norwell, Massachusetts 02061 USA
Telephone (781) 871-6600
Fax (781) 871-6528
E-Mail <kluwer@wkap.com>

Distributors for all other countries:
Kluwer Academic Publishers Group
Post Office Box 322
3300 AH Dordrecht, THE NETHERLANDS
Telephone 31 78 6576 000
Fax 31 78 6576 474
E-Mail <orderdept@wkap.nl>

   Electronic Services <http://www.wkap.nl>

Library of Congress Cataloging-in-Publication

SYNCHRONIZING E-SECURITY
by Godfried B. Williams
ISBN: 1-4020-7646-0

Dedications

To my wife, Sylvia, daughter, Maxine
and
In memory of my Uncle, Maxwell

CONTENTS

LIST OF FIGURES

LIST OF TABLES

LIST OF CONTRIBUTORS

Mr. Jamil Ampomah, Editing Consultant

Mr. Paul Victor Avudzivi, CEO, Dayspring Conglomerate

NOBA Research

Data Pro Ltd

Zeenext Ltd

Manipal Ltd

Soft Ltd

AT & T Global Network

MTNL Ltd

Afrisat Ltd

AST Ltd

Wang CSL

AOL

Preface

This book is a critical investigation and empirical analysis of studies conducted amongst companies that support electronic commerce transactions based in both advanced and developing economies. It presents insights into the validity and credibility of current risk assessment methods that support electronic transactions in the global economy. The book focuses on a number of case studies of IT companies in selected countries in West Africa, Europe, Asia and United States of America. The foundations of this work have been based on previous studies by Williams G., Avudzivi P.V (Hawaii 2002) on the retrospective view on information security management and the impact of Tele-banking on the End-user. Most leading IT companies in developing economies, purchase expensive equipment to ensure that services provided to organisations that exchange funds through electronic means become fully secured during transactions. The rational behind this hypothesis is based on the strong competition that exists among these leading IT companies. Contrary to companies in developing economies there has been a certain level of complacency amongst advanced economies, although some academics and practitioners might disagree with this view. The irony of this analysis is that, while investments in security amongst IT companies in advanced economies are not that high in budget, the methods employed for assessing possible risks in the application of technologies are normally high in cost. These investigations depict that elements and factors for risk assessment in developing and advanced economies are not usually met with appropriate counter measures or methods. I strongly believe that readers of this book will gain a detailed insight into the issues involved. A proposed guideline for ensuring the synchronisation of electronic security is also outlined. The audience of this book is postgraduate students undertaking research in internet security policies, algorithm design, risk assessment methods and strategic information systems planning. Final year courses in issues in distributed systems and internet engineering. Issues in information systems development and practice could be enhanced by some of the issues addressed in this book. It will also be an appropriate source of reference for MBA students reading information management, systems management and E-commerce as well as practitioners.

ACKNOWLEDGEMENTS

Thanks to my Editors Susan and Sharon for their consistent reminders and useful comments.

Many thanks to Mr Jamil Ampomah (Audit Consultant -Deutsche Telekom), for his detailed comments and diligent feedback on the entire manuscript. The personal sacrifice, commitment and diligence displayed were priceless. It is scintillating to note that after a period of 20 years when we were at high school, you have maintained such thoroughness in your approach to work.

My sincere thanks to Mr Paul-Victor Avudzivi(CEO-Dayspring Conglomerate), who contributed to the foundations of this work. Your input in the security of electronic business processes was very useful.

I will like to thank Mr. Murgesh of Manipal International Ltd, India for providing leads to information sources; AT&T Global networks South Africa, Mr. Bernard Bonney (CEO-NOBA research),Mr. Raymond Ankobia (ex Chief Programmer/Analyst SOFT Ltd), Mr. Mike Kagya(Systems Engineer –NCR/AT&T), AOL and all the anonymous reviewers and contributors

I will also like to acknowledge past experiences gained from my team members on the World Bank *AMISU project*. These experiences gave me insights into security issues related to the application of computers in a global context. They also served as motivations whilst pursuing this research work. Mr. Bruce Smith, Mr John Anthony, and Mrs Tay (Consultants-International Development Association of the World Bank – *AMISU project*),Dr. Gershon Adzadi (External Consultant-World Bank - *AMISU project*). Gershon, the word "procedures" always rung a bell and kept me going.

A special thank you to Mr A.Beckley of the European Union Agency for international fund disbursement.

My gratitude to colleagues at University of East London UK for their comments, especially, Dr. David Preston; your initial comments were helpful. Dr. Hossein Jahankhani; words like "this thing does not look nice" gave me second thoughts. Dr.Hamid Jahankhani, "How far with the book?" Mr.Kwame Kyei "I think human ware in network security is crucial".

Dr.Chris Imafidon, "whiz kid in MS tools", Mr Solomon Alexis and Mr Joseph Annan for your support. To Linda and Elaine your patience in answering some of my questions in word processing were appreciative.
Thanks to Elyas, my BSc. final year project student who collected data on students' profile.

Thanks to Professor Moti Yung (Adjunct research scientist -Columbia State University, New York USA) for useful suggestions and pointers, Professor Adel Elmargraby(University of Louisville, Kentucky, USA) ,Don Anderson (President - Quantum International Corporation, Louisville, Kentucky USA) for their keen interest and enthusiasm shown in this research work. I would like to thank Dr.Shukri Wakid (Senior Scientist-Hewlett-Packard, Gaithersburg, Maryland, USA) for comments on intelligent security in high performance computing.

My appreciation to my mother in law who babysat my daughter Maxine whilst writing this book.

To my mum, I say a big thank you for your inspiration, and to the special memories of my Father.

Chapter 1

Overview of technologies that support International banking

The major technologies used within Tele-banking are ATM (Automatic Tele Machines) for cash point withdrawals and other banking services, home banking using personal computers and accounting software packages linked remotely to banks by modems, the Internet as a platform for electronic commerce, EDI (Electronic Data Interchange) and the electronic wallet or purse. It must be noted that in as much as each is assessed on its own merit or demerit, they usually work in consonance with each other. The author has considered how each one has been subjected to various security infringements, analysed customers reaction towards them and suggested ways that when considered could enhance their functionality.

1.1 ATM (Automatic Teller Machine)

Looking at ATM specifically, most security problems have been related to the human aspect. As a result end-users have been educated by most bankers, concerning confidentiality of PIN (personal identification numbers) on their electronic cards. Security awareness of the ATM has mostly been passed on from the banker to the End-user. One way of ensuring control is by creating awareness in the End-user to change his PIN periodically. Although most banks have implemented such a system, which is user-friendly, it was observed that continuous end-user awareness has been generally absent. This aspect of Tele banking technology has improved in terms of its security system, precisely hardware controls. However more is left to be addressed. Possible infringements have been caused by negligence on the part of the End-user, by an unconscious disclosure of confidential information to anonymous persons. The other security issue possibly which bankers and End-users have not thought of, is whether all ATMs that we see in our communities and other places may not be "copy cats" of the actual one designed by criminals to capture confidential information about customers. If that is the case in present times, what verification or validation checks have bankers put in place to ensure that customers are able to verify whether their electronic cards are slotted into the correct machines?

Based on these current developments in End-user technology, it is very critical for Management of the banking industry to take adequate steps to ensure that appropriate implementation and control strategy are adopted.

1.2 Telephone and home banking

The next technology examined is Telephone and home banking. Some ten million people in the United States of America regularly use personal computers and financial management software packages such as intuits Quicken or Microsoft money to manage their chequebooks and reconcile their personal financial transactions Evans(1997).

As mentioned in previous paragraphs, current versions of these computer programs can use modems to access electronic switches operated by check-free or visa interactive, which in turn route instructions or queries to the customer's bank. Such a system makes customers pay bills, make transfers, receive electronic statements and seamlessly incorporate account data into their personal financial plans Evans (1997). Since home banking functions by using other technological platforms, such as the Internet, it should be noted that, apart from this ten million estimated people in America, who are quite comfortable with the system, most users of this type of banking facilities are quite sceptical about the security aspect of this technology.

This is due to the fact that, the Internet is not exclusively protected from criminals or hackers, neither do most telephone systems have cryptography facilities that could be used in encrypting telephone conversations. At least it is known that most End-users do not have such systems at their homes. There is a divided school of thought concerning the security of the technology, on one half is pro home banking and on the other half is anti home banking.

1.2.1 Advocates of home and telephone banking

The pro home banking believers advocate that the right technology, standards, policy and controls must be implemented to ensure it's current improvement and future perfection. In fact market research suggests that quicken users are more likely to be loyal to their software than to their Banks Evans (1997). This implies that End-users of the quicken software package may be in the position to migrate to another Bank where such a facility for home banking exist. The above test case still stands to be proven.

The views of the pro telephone bankers seem to be taken from the standpoint that appropriate certified software and easy to use tools encourage users to participate in telephone banking. Standardisation and proper certification of software tools according to the advocates promotes security. Notwithstanding these assertions there is still much to be desired when it comes to satisfactory security standards.

1.2.2 Sceptics of home and telephone banking

Financial fraud over the Internet is still relatively rare, but not unknown. A recent example was FORTUNA ALLIANCE, a fraudulent pyramid investment scheme based off-shore from America, but advertising its so called money making opportunity on an Australian website. It raked an estimated $9 million in five months before being shut down Jones (1997). Such an execution of fraud by a single syndicate is a significant loss from every economic and financial point of view. This is a typical case, where the End-user involved in home banking may be attracted to a financial service, supposedly a Bank, and through the internet websites go astray and become a victim of criminal activity of this kind. In analysing this case carefully, the end-user could be a loser in this instance. It is crystal clear that the Internet is highly vulnerable in security aspects concerning its use for Tele banking.

The Internet is further investigated as a technological platform used for distant banking and its security implications. Quoting Viscount Chelmsford, President of the electronic commerce association (ECA) in his article subtitled the true state of progress towards electronic commerce in the real world. " *I am a keen supporter of the growth of electronic commerce, however my initial welcome for the term, which led to change in the name of our association to that of electronic commerce association (ECA) soon turned sour" unquote.* He goes on to say "I am not alone in stating that this was "pain wrong". Solutions to the problems related to this technology are found in niche areas Chelmsford (1998).

In the process of looking at the issues that might have served as barriers, security was mentioned as a major one.

1.2.3 A case assessed by a UK Parliamentary group

Let us also consider the case of an ISP (Internet Service Provider) assessed at a meeting of Derek Wyatt MP's all party Internet group. This ISP sells new software across the Internet. Any consumer can buy any software he or she wants and download it but in an encrypted format. The End-user is instructed in clear language what to do in order to send payment card details back to the ISP using the same encryption. Such details are at risk across the Internet for about three seconds but are protected by the ISP's simple encryption. The question one may like to ask is, how can the End-user prove the integrity of the ISP since any criminal can equally design a web page, advertising brilliant facilities, only for the public to find out that it was all fraudulent, given the case above. Instead of the End-user thinking that the details passed on via the Internet to the service provider were not secured, he or she rather thought that the risk was between him and his bank. The Internet service provider was equally thinking along similar lines. The bank clears the amount owed and the service provider sends a message to the consumer and then allows him to decrypt his new software. When the service provider was asked what he was doing to encourage growth and improvement of the situation the service provider said "nothing" Chelmsford (1998).

1.2.4 The loose end of security

This is a clear example of a loose security problem within the Internet which present end users, may not be aware of, as such may be illusive of how their bank accounts might be secured. One of the security problems which Tele banking contends with using Internet as a platform for commercial transaction is the fact that, its present structure makes it difficult to detect theft of information and virtually impossible to trace tampering. Anyone can operate under a false identification.

The problem here is that break-ins, fraud, including theft are observed within the purview of Governmental agencies. Since various Governments have not been in the position to define what constitutes theft it becomes difficult to control such violations of security.

1.3 Electronic Wallet

The other technological area that is developing rapidly apart from Tele banking is the "electronic wallet or purse". Rymer Rigby highlights the fact that Mondex's master card has passed it's pilot test Rigby(1997). This depicts the fact that the electronic purse is a technology which shows signs of completely engulfing future financial transactions and a platform which will be used for transfer of funds between banks, customers and firms.

It is likely that two NatWest employees, Tim Jones and Graham Higgins had this technology in mind, when they begun looking at "smart cards" back in 1990. Smart cards as opposed to most other cards are based on magnetic chip technology. This was a development by NatWest in 1992. A year later Midland and NatWest announced that in conjunction with British Telecom, they would be launching a pilot scheme in Swindon. The basis for this further development was to improve on the security problems faced when using magnetic stripe technology. It must be noted that the development of this technology is still on-going as such has not reached the point of universal use.

Infact Peter Hill, a Mondex's chief technology officer and a VISA deserter points to the fact that the requisite security technologies resided on the chip, rather than externally, as has mostly been portrayed or claimed. This will allow safe transfer of funds over any insecure network.

The question which those with security phobia will ask is, are most present systems not still using the magnetic stripe technology? The answer will be yes. If that is true then they will be vindicated by other users who think that security within Tele banking faced by the end-user is still weak. In the UK, explains Ron Clark, head of Mondex UK (and one of the brains behind SWITCH) the 'roll out' period will be determined by the progress of the now inevitable move from magnetic strips to chips. There are all indications that in the UK and other European countries from 1998 to the early parts of the 21st century the banks will be moving from magnetic strips to magnetic chips, with those prone to fraud, such as the gold cards receiving more priority Rigby (1997).

1.3.1 How will the electronic wallet work?

As part of the radical vision of Internet commerce, the electronic wallet as a complementary technology will be full of electronic money. The manufacturing of electronic money quite depends on anonymous electronic notes. An organisation would sell the note to its customers, coding the electronic cash onto a Wallet sized card or sending it to another on-line merchant. It will debit the disbursed E-money plus a small transaction fee from customers' regular bank accounts. For this process to be successful the transfers must be anonymous and highly secured. Although it seems quite good and credible, security is not assured since there is no central authority of high and unquestionable integrity monitoring the system. This as a means of exchange still leaves "room" for further investigation and research. The other 'headache' with these technologies is that national Governments have little interest in taking on the problem, because electronic cash raises a lot of troubling law enforcement questions Spar., Bussgang(1996).

1.3.2 Get the first right or get all wrong

In fact the security of fund transfer and exchange should revolve around the following three sequential processes, namely authentication, approval and answerability. Among these three the most crucial is authentication. This is because throughout human history people have had the need to prove beyond reasonable doubt who they claim to be. This has been the first norm in effecting any financial transaction between people, companies and countries. It also assures the parties involved in the transaction that the entities participating in the business transaction are the rightful signatories. Approval and answerability are worthier if authentication is positive. In other words get the first right or get all wrong. It is in this spirit and letter that this book treats the subject of authentication in financial transactions by critically assessing the technologies that support the process. Approval and answerability are not dealt with in detail in this book, since it is the author's view that both are secondary to authentication. In other words the book discusses authentication as the critical aspect of security.

1.4 Authentication

Authenticating transactions from developing economies can not also be guaranteed. This is due to the fact that certification bodies in advanced economies such as UK and USA do not put into global context the digital certificates that are designed and issued. This is not just having confidence and assurance in the software used by these leading IT companies for businesses in these developing economies, but also strongly engaging IT companies in these economies to contribute to the standardisation and certification of the products they consume. It is no wonder that EU legislation prohibits persons and businesses alike from engaging in electronic business across the Atlantic and Pacific. There is also a missing consortium of businesses that have signed up to any form of trust or certification as a means of authenticating business transactions globally among for example West African communities. The author's views from these findings are that the elements and factors required for risk assessment do not lie within the technical framework of security, such as hardware or software firewalls. Issues such as encryption and decryption algorithms are equally secondary. The risk assessment methods should rather be focused on soft issues related to structure of organisation, communication, financial strength and capabilities and technical expertise which in most cases is neither available nor can be afforded.

1.4.1 A major issue in authentication

One of the major issues which were difficult to understand from the global economic point of view was the way advanced economies' policies, laws and directives discouraged individual businesses from transacting business with less advanced economies, due to the high risk associated with the businesses located in weaker economies. This is not a realistic option in a world where there is interdependency. It is also not plausible in the sense that the Internet and the Web have bridged the gap between nations and subsequently made communications simpler and easier. The disable is able, the weak is now strong due to the upsurge of information distribution. It is also not prudent to extricate business communications that have been established between the companies within these economies. The next section is an overview and assessment of methods used in authentication.

1.5 Techniques, Methods and Technologies used in authentication of electronic transactions.

This section classifies authentication into three categories, namely human to human, human to system and system to system. The author has described them as user authentication and system authentication. The reason for these three categories is based on the premise that authentication is a multidirectional or multidimensional activity.

The purpose of this section is to present the reader with the most common methods applied and current trends in authentication methods and how each affects the transactions we make through electronic means.

Figure 1 - Categories of authentication methods

Types of Authentication	Human to Human	Human to System	System to System
Mutual Authentication	√	√	
Digital Certificates	√		
User Identification and names		√	
Passwords		√	
Profiling		√	
Biometrics		√	
Token allocation			√
CHAP(Challenge Handshake Authentication Protocol)			√
Kerberos			√
Intelligent Agents			√

1.6 Human to Human authentications

Human in this context refers to person, group of people and organisations. This section discusses mutual authentication and digital certificates as aspects of human to human authentication.

1.6.1 Mutual Authentication

This is when two people or a person and a system engage in an electronic communication in order to verify the identity of the other. An example that shows person to person or person to system is the customer and bank relationship. A clerk at the bank will ensure that a customer possesses identification, which is consistent with the information held about the customer by the bank. This information could either be the date of birth or mother's maiden name. The other example is a customer who interacts with an automated system by telephone or Internet to confirm unique personal details before the system grants approval and access to, for instance current balance.

1.6.1.1 Electronic banking standards and mutual authentication

Appropriate banking standards, especially international banking does not allow any form of transfer of funds to be carried by telephone; however these standards do not apply fully when it comes to transfer by the internet. The problem associated with this form of authentication is a challenging one. This is because persons at remote geographical locations crossing national boundaries with personal details of an electronic crime victim could without any sweat transfer funds from one account to another. Although there are numerous computer security fraternities with computer experts, it is generally believed that there are sceptics amongst these groups when it comes to transacting any form of business on the Internet, especially when the business is across the Atlantic or Pacific. The reasons for this are mainly technical. One wonders how many switches and gateways credit card details might travel through in order for it to arrive at the appropriate destination or recipient.

1.6.1.2 The encryption argument

Although personal details sent across the Internet are encrypted, encryption could either be end to end or link to link encryption. The end to end encryption is commonly used since it is cheaper whiles link to link encryption is rarely used because it is very expensive. The rational conclusion to draw here is that most companies will adopt the former since the prime object of most companies is to make profit and not maximise productivity. We will be kidding ourselves and having a false sense of security if we think otherwise. This affects confidentiality and integrity pertaining to the security layers that the information must travel through before getting to its' final destination. The layers the Information travel through are dynamic and not static. The dynamic routing of information is considered because service providers will like to optimise the efficiency of their business transactions, therefore there is a trade off between efficiency and security, since the less congested routes on the Internet might not be secured. This implies that personal details from credit cards in the form of information packets could be sniffed or eavesdropped from the internet using for instance specialised sniffing software in the form of intelligent agents.

1.6.1.3 Implications of the lack of comprehensive encryption procedures

The absence of comprehensive encryption procedures could cause an eavesdropper to use sniffing software to download information from the Internet. This could be used to effect an Internet transaction by adopting the profile of the victim whose personal details were eavesdropped. The pro Internet security gurus might disagree with this assertion, however it is believed undoubtedly that there are security flaws when it comes to ensuring the integrity and confidentiality of credit card details sent across the Internet. A recent documentary on credit card fraud was presented on a BBC Channel on the 20th of May 2003. An expert in credit card security admitted that there were still major lapses in credit card security, due mainly to the fact that most banks have not migrated from the magnetic strip to the magnetic chip. His reasons were that although credit cards embedded with magnetic Chips were more secured the cost of implementing the technology was more expensive. His conclusions were that since the total cost of security flaws was less than implementing this technology, then from a financial point of view it was more appropriate and sustainable to maintain the current technology.

1.6.2 Digital Certificates

These are used in the authentication of a person's or an organisation's digital identity during an electronic transaction. This could be used during the sending of emails or an electronic fund transfer. This again is usually combined with cryptography technologies such as encryption and digital signatures. It is mostly between individuals or organisations; however it is effectively implemented by the inclusion of a third party who confirms the legitimacy of the parties involved. There is an issue of trust when it comes to certification. This is discussed in more detail in chapter 3 under the sub-heading policies and standards.

1.7 (HSA) Human to System authentication

A system here refers to the hardware, software and process components of a computer and its' processing environment. This section discusses the use of user identification and names, passwords, profiling and biometrics as methods of authentication.

1.7.1 User Naming and Identification

This is a unique identification used by humans to identify them to personal computers, computer networks and multiple networks or distributed platforms. It could be in any form; however it is more logical to use names that have some personal relation to the user of that system. The common form of username is the first name of the user. It could also be some family related name or a nickname. It is important to realise that it is part of the authentication process and should be accorded some degree of importance as any form of authentication. User names and identifications should not be publicly accessible or seen by third parties. Making them accessible by other unauthorised persons weakens the processes of authentication in the layers of security.

The obtaining of user names and identification by unauthorised persons is one step forward in adopting a victim's profile. It provides a basis for masquerading. Masquerading is when one entity pretends to be a different entity Stallings (2003). This form of Masquerading could take place in the banking environment. Unauthorised users could informally attain details of customers' profile and use it for criminal activities. This is discussed in detail in section 1.7.2. Another example is enabling a member of staff of an organisation with limited database rights to obtain additional access rights by impersonating another member of staff with special administrative rights.

1.7.2 Password

This is a series of characters which when combined with a username or identification authenticates the user of a system. The password should be handled with high importance. An effective security system will encourage users to change passwords periodically. This is because passwords could be guessed based on probabilities and also an understanding of the profiles of computer system users. For instance, a person with very deep interest in religious matters is likely to use adjectives and nouns such as holy, law, love, prophet, preacher etc. A politically minded person might use words like justice, election, government, policy or vote. This is at the primary stage. A secondary stage will be a combination of these words and some form of pneumonic. The most advance stage is a word that depicts the direct opposite of the interest of such persons. It should be understood here that, password systems as a means of authentication are not only applied in the context of Human Computer Interactions. Most banks demand a form of password when a customer attempts to withdraw funds at the counter. The password system is normally based on a set of routine or generic questions such as, *mother's maiden name, work telephone number, home telephone number, type of personal bank card, previous home address, post code etc.* These seem to be the commonest questions that are asked by most national and international banks. Such password systems are easily to break because the banks rarely implement a policy that informs the customer to make changes to password systems that match with their profile. This type of *authentication* process and concept is usually transferred to Internet banking in an automated form. The probability that such systems are broken into is very high. Intruders and hackers do not need the mind of a genius to violate the security of such systems. This is because such personal information is not difficult to acquire. Information for violating password systems could be acquired through the following channels: *Grapevine (informal channels of communication), advance search and queries on the Internet, Search in Garbage cans, bins in residential areas, through fake sales representative and provision of incentives to people during data collection exercises.*

It is important for banks to take seriously the problem areas highlighted in order to respond to the existing security threats discussed.

1.7.3   Profiling

In this section I introduced profiling as a research technique that vaguely has it's roots from the discipline of user modelling a decade ago (Webb et al, 2001). It has been used in a number of applications and disciplines ranging from computer user interface design and customer profiling in the retail industry under the guise of user modelling (Webb et al, 2001). A major application area is adaptive systems. This area of research applies profiling in the personalisation of individuals by demonstrating how it could be applied as a useful tool as part of the authentication process in electronic transactions. It also shows that it could be employed as a tool in computer forensics by unveiling the hidden identities of persons who use the Internet or any form of global electronic communication device. Although some authors classify profiling under the study of biometrics, the author believes it should be dealt under the category of behavioural science rather than physical science. This suggests that the various definitions given to biometrics should be reassessed. The author believes that biometrics in its simplest definition is the study of the measurements of physical attributes and characteristics of living organisms rather than the attributes and characteristics of behaviour of these organisms. Examples of these are the iris and retinal patterns, hand geometry and the characteristics of the face. Studies recently conducted among 200 students at the University of East London, UK have been analysed using a spreadsheet and a Kohonen neural architecture to illustrate how profiling could aid authentication. See further analysis under objectives of studies.

1.7.3.1 Objectives of studies

The purpose of the studies was to bring to light how profiling could be used as an effective method in authentication.

The investigations showed how students of the university used their computer network account. The data collected were analysed and broken down into different data sets and subsequently fed into a neural network program. The neural network revealed different behavioural patterns among students. These patterns appeared as clusters representing the profile categories that existed amongst the students after the analysis of the results

1.7.3.2 Methodology

Questionnaires were used to collect information from 200 students. The students were placed into two categories. Students reading technical degrees (i.e. IT,

Engineering, Electronics, Architecture etc.) and non technical degrees (i.e. Sociology, law, language studies etc).

1.7.3.3 Analysis of results

Figure 2

Kohonen Network Viewer				
	var_0001	var_0002	var_0003	var_0004
Node 5	39.539959	42.96209	55.11219	41.197746
Node 6	38.597641	39.925724	54.431625	40.464828
Node 7	38.0	28.502365	33.505096	31.502111
Node 8	38.0	36.517101	50.800064	38.673199
Node 9	23.831259	4.715504	15.95293	26.424389
Node 10	30.179852	28.789875	39.887737	30.524605
Node 11	36.841034	37.647682	50.804211	38.146759

1.7.3.4 Analysis of Kohonen Network

Figure 2 is a cluster diagram derived from the Kohonen neural network architecture. The cluster diagram shows that there are mainly five (5) types of profiles at the highest level. These are based on the main clusters that constitute the diagram. A detailed analysis also depicts that there are sixty-four (64) different clusters concentrated amongst the five cluster regions identified.

The clustered diagram was based on analysis of data extracted from a spreadsheet. The data extracted from the spreadsheet was fed into the neural network for training. The objective of the neural network training was to reveal a more detail picture and a true classification of the profiles that existed based on the results of the survey. Although it is not the subject of this book to map the 64 classes of profiles unto their characteristics, it however reaffirms to a high extent the power of profiling. The application of appropriate and reliable data sets, based on a real life study in the personalisation of persons provides useful results. The studies for instance shows that among the 200 student respondents there were approximately

25% of persons whose profiles were similar or the same in each of the groupings. See high level analysis of Table 1. The result was to determine the profiles that existed amongst the students. There was no test for linkage between for instance course and student profile. This could have been interesting as an area of further analysis.

Table 1 (Describes 4 main profiles that evolved in the study)

Group 1	Group 3
Interest in Internet News = High Interest in Entertainment=High Interest in Sports=High Frequency of Internet Usage = High Frequency of email usage=High	Interest in Internet News = Low Interest in Entertainment=High Interest in Sports=High Frequency of Internet Usage = High Frequency of email usage=High
Group 2 Interest in Internet News = Low Interest in Entertainment=High Interest in Sports=Low Frequency of Internet Usage = High Frequency of email usage=High	Group 4 Interest in Internet News = High Interest in Entertainment=Low Interest in Sports=High Frequency of Internet Usage = High Frequency of email usage=High

1.7.4 Biometrics

Authenticating electronic transactions using the measurement of physical attributes of a person is biometrics. The physical attributes are normally derived from the following features; Fingerprint; Facial geometry; Iris pattern; Retina; Hand geometry; Finger geometry; Vein structure of back of hand; Ear form; Voice; DNA; Odour or Gait etc. The discussion in this book has been based on the most common features that are usually tested.

1.7.4.1 How does Biometrics work?

A physical characteristic of a person is captured; information captured is input in software that creates a template of the characteristic captured; the template created is secured in a repository. This could be an electronic chip or a smart card. A life scan of the captured information is matched unto the stored biometrics feature; A matching score is derived based on the criteria specified for identification and verification whiles an audit trail is used to occasionally verify the reliability of the system. The implications of using this technology are enormous; these are related to cost and versatility of the technology. The problem of versatility relates to the ability to move the technology around just to satisfy a few individuals who want to effect a transaction. This could also affect for instance company staff who might be carrying out transactions on behalf of their companies globally regardless of geographical locations. This is because making biometrics information available on distributed platforms has risk implications. There are also aspects of the technology that is not yet advanced to deal with issues regarding versatility.

1.8 (SSA) System to system authentication

This section is a discussion on CHAP and Kerberos authentication processes. SSA is referred as the authentication process between two or more computers or network systems. This is also referred to as end to end or node to node authentication. A typical example of such authentication mechanism is the (CHAP) Challenge handshake authentication protocol.

1.8.1 (CHAP)Challenge handshake authentication protocol

CHAP is a Point to Point Protocol (PPP). The objective of CHAP is to ensure that end to end systems or node to node that communicate with each other are authentic and legitimate. The main object of CHAP is to ensure that computer or end systems on any network are qualified to be part of a particular communication process within the network Campbell.,Calvert,Boswell(2003).

Phases in CHAP challenge and reply process are as follows:

1. The node or an end system asks the authenticating server if it can use CHAP.
2. The authenticating server replies, telling the end system that it can use CHAP.
3. The authenticating server sends a challenge message to the end system.
4. The node replies with a value that has been calculated with a hash function.

5. The authenticating node receives the reply and checks it against its own calculation of the expected hash value.
6. The authentication sends a new challenge to the node in a sparing manner throughout the entire network.
7. The receiving node or end system should then respond to the challenge

Masquerading, spoofing and traffic analysis could be used by attackers and hackers of the system to make the authentication process vulnerable. These are issues that have to be dealt with on a global scale. Unless the technologies for supporting authentication processes are opened to developing and advanced economy computer system platforms, transactions will be vulnerable to threat, from a global perspective.

1.8.2 Kerberos authentication process

Kerberos authentication process was designed at the Massachusetts Institute of Technology (MIT). This section is an examination of some of the assumptions based upon which the authentication system operates, rather than looking at the technical rigour of the way it works. The reasons for this approach are that the assumptions become a good basis for assessing the areas of danger and threat in the technology.

1.8.3 Assumptions

*   Denial of service attacks are not built into the system therefore are not prevented

Denial of service is a direct attack on the services of network. This is when an attacker prevents the services of a network reaching its customers or clients. It can be very costly. It is not every security system that could prevent denial of service, as a result using Kerberos authentication is equally subject to danger. This assumption also suggests that there should be some level of personal responsibility in ensuring security of any authentication process during the transferring of funds electronically.

*   Password guessing is handled by the system

Section 1.7.2 discussed issues related to password systems. One of the main problems regarding password systems implemented by banks was the fact that, the profile of persons formed part of the reasoning behind password

18

systems. The investigations also showed that the range of questions that constituted password systems were a few. The assumption made here by the Kerberos authentication process will be a means of weakness. This is because discussions in section 1.7.2 and 1.7.3 show that not all password systems are guessed. Some password systems are engineered and well orchestrated as part of the execution process.

- Passwords must be kept secret.

How secret are passwords? Is there anything secret under the sun? The assessment of password systems show that password systems at counter level and Internet banking systems could be violated as a result of the reasons speculated in section 1.7.2. The Kerberos authentication process and other authentication processes should enforce a policy of password management system that reminds users of Internet banking systems to make changes to their passwords.

- It assumes that all network devices physically connected to the network are secured.

One would have thought that a better way of providing security for a system is to rather assume that network devices physically connected to a network are not secured. This could help an authentication process such as Kerberos to facilitate intrusion detection. Intrusions could be detected at access points of network devices that are not well secured. The inverse of Kerberos assumption will handle both secured and non-secured part of the network.

- Internal clocks used for authentication must be loosely synchronised.

Synchronisation of internal clocks is a process where the computer clocks in a local area network or sub-net are harmonised such that they fall in line with other external clocks globally. This enables authentication to take place successfully without discrepancies in global timing.

1.8.4 Summary of Chapter 1

This chapter provided an overview of the background of technologies that support electronic transactions within the framework of international banking. The impact of security on the end user has been discussed with particular emphasis on the weaknesses that exist in the technologies used in home banking, electronic wallet, electronic fund transfer and the Internet. Authentication methods that assure the legitimacy of an electronic transaction have been brought to light. These methods form the critical phase of any security system. This is because it upholds the three main goals of security, integrity, availability and confidentiality. Authentication verifies the truth regarding the nature of any electronic transaction. This is what makes the process important in the goal of integrity. Breaking the confidentiality of any financial transaction could sometimes be achieved if the identification and verification processes within authentication are not met with the appropriate counter measures. This in effect makes information regarding a particular transaction available to unscrupulous persons, as a result breaching another key goal in security.

Chapter 2

Manpower

(Technical and Non Technical support for e-security)

In this chapter technical and non-technical manpower available in supporting new security technologies are examined. Particular emphasis is placed on level of expertise and training received by people who either manage or use these systems.

2.1 Background

"In a world where risk surrounds businesses at all times, it's more important than ever to have an accurate assessment of that risk. We can never eliminate risk, but we can manage and control it" Mestchian (2003).

Eliminating risk is virtually impossible since every decision we take in every day life has a relative risk that has to be dealt with. Whether we deal with the risk successfully or not depends on our understanding of the implicated risk from our decisions. The manpower in most organisations has it's own perceptions of risk. Judgements made on the application of laid down procedures within the organisation to ensure secured systems are dependent on the perception of risk by individuals who constitute the manpower. This is also affirmed by Mestchian(2003). He highlights people failure in organisations. According to his studies people within or outside the organisation could cause this failure. This could be done either deliberately or accidentally. Due to this phenomenon it is important to ensure that people who interact with these systems are adequately trained. People within the organisation could always receive training. What is missing is the lack of training given to End-users Williams.,Avudzivi (2002). The Orange Phone Company in the United Kingdom for instance makes training available to its' customers in usability optimisation Orange (2003). The training is a way of helping customers to make efficient and effective use of their mobile phones. This seems to be a step in the right direction. Conversely information provided to customers who interact with banking systems is inadequate.

2.2 A UK and USA survey on why cryptographic systems fail

This study conducted by Ross Anderson shows the importance of human ware in security systems.

The studies highlighted the failure modes of retail banking systems, which constituted the largest application of cryptography. According to the studies failures were not caused by crypt-analysis or other technical attacks, but by implementation mistakes and management failures. Such is the fallible nature of man. We can always get some things right but we can not always get all things right. The problems outlined above are all human related. If we can invest more in the manpower and human ware whether internal or external of our organisations we will be able to improve security. The situation in developing economies is worse, although systems in developing economies are equally sophisticated. The *bandwagon syndrome* makes IT firms and Government institutions approve the purchasing of these systems at sometimes economically outrageous prices. It is however unfair to generalise that all decisions are based on this *bandwagon syndrome*. A small percentage of these systems are subject to appropriate evaluations before any purchase is done. It is rather the continuous maintenance of these systems in terms of risk and vulnerability that is lacking. Prior to the Internet era, electronic fraud in developing economies was uncommon. The technologies that supported such transactions were mediocre. The tide has changed in recent times. The technologies available to most major institutions in developing economies that commit themselves to business transactions abroad meet proprietary international standards. It is the human ware that needs to be looked at by injecting best practice standards into these economies.

2.3 Perspective from developing economies

The assessment of technical support is usually unsatisfactory. Technical manpower is quite expensive for companies and businesses that employ the technologies sold to them. In some best efforts, the IT vendors attempt to train local members of the company to assume these roles. Investigations conducted by Dayspring Conglomerate reveal that the percentage of (SME) Small and Medium Enterprises that attempt to use the Internet for example in business transactions mostly opt for a cheaper option. This results in serious security implications. Alternative support is provided by the leading IT companies. This also causes the SME to excessively rely on the IT companies and subsequently expose them to security risks.

2.4 *Below are some companies in Ghana (West Africa) that have a high investment in IT infrastructure with particular emphasis on security. These are among companies floated on the local and international stock exchanges. They have a high level of participation in international trade.*

- Ashanti Goldfields Co. Ltd
- Standard Chartered Bank Ghana Ltd
- Unilever Ghana Ltd
- Ghana Commercial Bank

Investigations conducted, reported in (chapter 4), indicated that these companies were supported by IT consulting firms locally and internationally based with subsidiaries in Ghana. Companies such as Delloitte and Touche, PriceWaterhouseCoopers, Soft Ltd, NOBA research and Dayspring Conglomerate have niche markets in the West Africa sub-region. These IT companies supported operational, middle and strategic management activities by providing (MIS) management information systems services via system and software tools. The expertise required in supporting these companies is very expensive taking into consideration current global economic conditions as a whole.

The modus operandi of these companies varies from one company to another. This raises issues related to standards and policies supporting certification of software products. There is also no central or independent body that approves or certifies the security aspects of software delivered. The systems are either normally shaped in brand or company names; this is very typical of multi-national companies with subsidiaries in the sub region. This criticism is not levelled at the companies as a way of questioning the quality of the software delivered. It is rather intended to expose the lack of synergy that exist between multi national consulting firms and software companies that operate both at the local and sub-regional level in Africa. The purpose of choosing some of the IT companies in Ghana for this study revolves around the Country's 2020 vision economic programme. The aim of the programme is for the economy of the country to reach middle income level by 2020, through primarily economic reforms and Information engineering with Technology.

Technical expertise supporting information services to ensure appropriate security standards are not adequate. The implication is that demand for these technical skills out weighs the supply of the required skill set. The companies have been classified into two groups. These are service providers and service subscribers. The service providers are the IT companies whiles the subscribers are the companies that are listed in section **2.4**. The following technical expertise of service providers was assessed for this project;

Network security management, Network programming, Network security configuration and Network operating systems security.

- Windows systems security
- Unix security
- Novel network security
- Cisco Technology security

The result of this assessment is documented in section 4.2.5.

2.5 Labour statistics on (ICT) Information and Communication Technology

ILO labour statistics also depict significant ICT manpower in both developing and advanced economies. For instance in Romania, employee numbers in ICT related jobs in 1999 rose from 15,000 to 17600 in year 2000 ILO (2002). The current market reflects such consistent growth in this sector. The average number of people employed by companies that provided ICT services with links abroad was 100 in Romania. The skills of these people met basic technical requirements and standards. This was based on the perception of standards in Romania. The report did not highlight any immediate concerns regarding levels of skills. The studies in Ghana also showed similar patterns in the area of competence and concerns. In Slovenia there are also approximately 80,000 Teleworkers. This reflects 8% of active members of the working population. This figure is quite significant, in the sense that 8% of the labour force will be making a considerable economic contribution. The following are the number distributions of Teleworkers manpower: 30,000 employees telework at home; 10,000 employees telework as self employed persons; 15,000 employees telework as mobile workers and 25,000 telework at less than 8 hours per week. The importance of this statistical breakdown is to help to envisage the variety of skill set that might evolve from these employees who use computers and mobile devices to work from remote geographical locations without encountering any connectivity problem. The issues and problems relating to the Slovenia work force is not one related to connectivity to remote computers. It is speculated from the ILO research that issues and problems relating to standardisation, skill set of technical and non-technical manpower supporting these teleworkers could be areas associated with risk. This will require effective security standards management.

ILO (2002). This is also an evidence of significant number of employees in the computer industry. Although this might reflect a high level representation, it provides an indication of number trends in the ICT sector. The cases considered in both advanced and developing economies show that ICT are used in similar context. There is also an indication of a gap in technical and non technical manpower. The management of teleworking for instance was highlighted as an area of concern. (See details of ILO statistics on Labour).

2.6 Summary of chapter 2

Chapter 2 provided a brief insight of the technical and non-technical manpower that supported e-security. It was highlighted in this chapter that human ware was an important and critical aspect of security in information systems. Manpower in most organisations perceived risk differently due to culture and the environment within which these systems were implemented. It was learnt that judgements made on the importance of laid down procedures for ensuring risk prevention were dependent on individuals within organisations. There is also disparity in skills possessed by manpower in developing and advanced economies. Implementation and management mistakes were also identified as causes of security failure.

Chapter 3

Risk Assessment, Policies and Standards

3.1 Risk assessment methods in information security management

This chapter highlights the role of risk assessment methods in the review of risk related to management information systems. Thus, risk assessment methodologies and exercises that are conducted on information systems security. The primary task here is to understand the processes and stages generally involved in implementing an *(ISMS) information security management system.*

The economic aspects of security and how it affects risk is further examined by considering why investment in risk assessment spending is far higher than risk prevention technologies.

The subsequent section investigates how policies and standards affect security information systems and their risk implications.

In implementing ISMS there are a number of important stages that a system developer in conjunction with a client, thus the user of the system should take into consideration. These stages are considered in the next section.

3.1.1 Proposed stages in implementing ISMS

1. Purchase a security standard

In deciding to purchase any standard the buyer should think about the following questions:

- What set of standards will be appropriate for the client. Does the standard support companies across developing and advanced countries? The assertion made here is that such questions have not been addressed in a satisfactory manner as evidenced by empirical studies in chapter 4.
- What is the cost of purchasing the standards?

2. Train personnel of client to implement security standard.

    - The forms in which this training should take in different economies have not been properly designed, therefore adopting and tailoring a training strategy in your particular circumstance as a client is necessary.

3. Assemble a team and agree on a strategy

    - A team should be assembled and a strategy agreed upon to move the system forward in the long term. This should be between 10-20 years, since this will integrate and cover the corporate strategy of the organisation. The recommended duration is based on the assumption that existing systems will be adapted to incorporate new security measures as part of the evolution of the system.

4. Make an assessment of the risk

    - Carry out a risk assessment by conducting an investigation into potential areas of risk. The areas of potential risk could be Physical (Hardware) devices, Logical (Software tools), Processes or human. This is detailed in section 3.1.2.

5. Design a document that outlines the policies of the system.

    - The policy document should reflect procedures for resolving problems that might evolve during the lifetime of the system. The type of assets available to the (MIS) management information system function should be documented and regularly updated. An audit of the assets is important. The audit could be carried out using an audit trailing system that will periodically or routinely run a check on the state of the assets.

6. Choose a registrar to certify the system

- An internationally recognised registrar should then be chosen to certify the system. The key issue here is the fact that a number of problems are associated with certification of systems and computer products. Some of the problems may relate to the integrity and credibility of the body that awards the certification. Although some organisations standards have gained international acceptance, coverage and participation of such standards is skewed towards advanced economies. Example of such an organisation is the BSI (British standard Institute).

3.1.2 Making an assessment of the risk

The risk assessment could be based on the following parameters or criteria.

- Identify ISMS assets, cost and importance
- Identify potential (SWOT) strengths, weaknesses, opportunities, threats and requirements related to these assets
- Define levels of vulnerabilities and threats
- Calculate the risk of exposure of the assets and the resulting business impact. This is usually based on probability and cost benefit analysis
- Generate a list of system risks
- Use modelling & simulation software tools at this stage to simulate the model depicting a real life environment

3.1.3 Synchronising e-risk.

- This could be addressed by management. There should be procedures outlined for handling the identified risk after the assessment
- It is important that exceptional controls are implemented in order that the risks identified are managed effectively
- A gap analysis has to be conducted in order to harmonise the difference risk elements in both developing and advanced computer network platforms
- Modelling and Simulation on empirical analysis(see chapter 5)

3.1.4 Risk management

In risk management one needs to look at a process of *identifying potential areas of risk, analyse the risk* and make an assessment or evaluation of the type and level of risk that has been identified. It is important to realise that risk is relative and subjective. The element of risk is usually dependent on the type of system and the application with which that system is being applied. For example the availability of customer profiles to retail companies might be classified as an area of low risk. This is because customer profiles available to companies and eavesdropped by third parties with criminal abilities might only be used for marketing purposes in order for a particular competitor to outwit other competitors on the market. On the contrary making profile information of clients of banks available to third parties could be considered a high risk. This is because analysis of profiles of bank customers by third parties who possess criminal tendencies could be used as a means of impersonation.

A risk assessment method such as SCERT (Synergistic Contingency Evaluation and Review Technique) for instance uses four stages to define the boundary of risk. These are:

- Identifying areas of activities, risks and responses
- Structuring the risks and responses by identifying specific and general responses leading to properly defined risks
- Identifying parameters which will serve as a yard stick for judging the outcome
- Manipulating and interpreting estimates based on probabilities of associated risks and costs. A contingency plan is devised to support the process

SCERT and other risk assessment methods and models have intrinsic generic assessment capabilities. Inasmuch as these generic methods could be adopted and adapted in different circumstances, customising a general purpose model as a tool for assessing the risks of an information system is not a simple and methodical task. The reasons are that, the environment where the system is being implemented is not one that could be controlled. The variables that are modelled and simulated are usually based on the assumptions that they will be controlled variables in the method of application. Variables evolving from unexpected disaster, market fluctuations, economic instability and retention of manpower can not be easily modelled due to their dynamic nature. Although some game theory simulators attempt to achieve this goal, the philosophical foundations are unstable due to the fact that they are not environmentally endemic and inclusive by nature. In other words they can not cope with fluid conditions.

3.1.5 Addressing the risk

As part of the management of risk it is important to have a means of **addressing the risk.** The availability of risk management models in the form of software tools suggests that the treatment of risk is swift. This is not however the case as most risk assessment tools lack the dynamism and reasoning that is required within different economies.

In addressing the risk, what management measures do you put in place to control the elements of risk within a particular organisation in a developing or advanced economy? The economy of scales and the indexes for measuring levels of importance and priority are different. An example is the World Bank's report on the Y2K millennium bug that highlighted measures that were not put in place in developing countries. The author's interpretation of the overall report is that advanced economies at that time underestimated the operational day to day requirements of the systems that functioned in developing economies. This is because they were not well-informed of the fact that most essential facilities such as electricity, manufacturing, agriculture and banking were supported by computer systems in these economies therefore the failure of these systems to function would have had catastrophic consequences on the entire global economy. There were companies that derived economic sustenance and benefits from electricity.

Before proceeding to look at the data gathered on the Y2K risk assessment, it would be appropriate to look at some economic implications of security. It should be noted that the subject of economics is a highly subjective one. A set of economic principles that might be highly successful in one country could fail terribly in another. A classical example is the economic policies that are recommended by international institutions such as the International Monetary Fund (IMF) and the World Bank which have not yet gained footing and made significant impact in most developing economies. We could speculate on numerous reasons why this is the case. Since the application of contemporary economic principles are not culture bound, it would be wise to conclude from a systems theory point of view rather than the theories of economics that, economics and culture are inseparable. This is because every culture is part of an economy whiles every economy is part of a culture, however not every economy is part of every culture and not every culture is part of every economy. Ross Anderson for instance speculates that incentives and security are correlated Anderson (1994). This might be true when it comes to advanced economies. His studies concentrated on U.S.A and UK. It should be emphasised that IT companies and banks in developing economies will not be able to provide incentives to their customers as a means of reducing risk. Developing economies do not have the economic power to provide such incentives.

3.2 The economics of security

This section is an assessment of the economics of security. The author's analysis has been based on the principles that govern micro and macroeconomics. Microeconomics relates to the study of decisions made by individuals regarding day to day activities, whiles macroeconomics deals with the dynamism within an economy as a whole. It relates to all entities in a nation, country or region. Although there are general economic principles and theories that apply to most countries and nations, it will not be prudent for us to think that these economic principles are a panacea to the problems of every country. It will be wrong for any economist to think that way. This is because factors such as financial power, culture Adams (1999), government policy, law, state of technology and manpower could indirectly make a potent economic strategy impotent. In other words these factors drive an economy. For instance manpower is the sustenance of any economy as discussed in chapter 2. If the manpower that sustains the dynamisms of growth is poor the growth of that economy might retard. It could also be speculated that security is dependent on how an economy is managed.

3.2.1 Equilibrium and economics of security

A quick glance at the global economy reveals that there is no balance or equilibrium Akerlofi, G.A (1970); this is because the economies of scale are wide apart. This kind of global state serves as a blueprint for global electronic security. It shows that global electronic security is not in equilibrium. It has been highlighted that global electronic security needs synchronization. In other words there is a gap that needs to be closed in order for all economies to enjoy some relative security globally. This gap can not be closed in the short and mid term since the economies of scale between developing and advanced economies are far apart. Engaging developing economies in a more effective way in international security policy design is the key to global electronic and information security. A classical example of an organisation that adopts such an approach to information security policy is the United Nations. One wonders what principle, theory and idea the seating of the permanent council is based upon. It demonstrates a lack of synergy of what actually provides the pivot for global security. There is marginal representation and membership of developing countries. It is just like saying we are all equal however some are more equal than others. This approach to international security policy design could be deemed as the Omnipotent, Omnipresent and Omniscient security policy and standard approach. This will often have catastrophic consequences in this electronic and information age.

3.2.2 Lessons from Vulkan

Lessons learnt from Vulkan (2003), in his book the economics of e-commerce, relating to what designers need to think about when designing products for e-commerce are shared here.

1. He states from his studies that "Any product or service can be traded in an electronic exchange as long as it can be standardised".

2. Standardisation is not simple. Even if the product itself is, or can be, standard, issues such as loyalty, reputation and security of long term contracts are likely to affect the decisions of participants to trade through the exchange.

The importance placed on standardisation is not something new. The credibility of his studies highlights the rationalisation of such standards in the market place. The author's contribution to his work relates to how you define this market place. At the beginning of this section it was mentioned that there were diverse economies across the globe. These economies operate on factors that are equally diverse. This suggests that the risks associated with e-commerce in developing economies are very different from that of advanced economies. Lack of understanding of these risks has contributed to the paradox in risk spending.

3.2.3 How do risk and fraud relate to economics?

An examination of several fraud cases in the United Kingdom concluded that most fraud committed were caused by human error Anderson (1994); Varian (2000). This according to the studies was due to the fact that most of the local banks were not serious in dealing with security related issues. The studies showed that in Britain if a dispute occurred between a bank and a customer the bank was always right unless the customer proved the bank wrong. This is a colossal task for the customer. Most customers are too busy to contend a dispute with a Bank. On the contrary in the USA if there was a dispute between a customer and a Bank, the onus was on the Bank to prove the customer wrong. This approach created some form of incentive for the Banks. It had a positive effect on the reduction of fraud Anderson (1994). The approach adopted by the USA demonstrated principles of economic liability. It was seen to be important to assign liability to the Bank, since it contributed to risk reduction. This also demonstrates that there is some form of value placed on customers by their respective Banks in USA. It also suggests that some form of incentive should be given to the party responsible for managing risk during transactions. The revelations from the studies will be however more useful in advanced economies; the same can not be said of developing economies. This is because developing economies do not have the economic strength to initiate policies that provide incentives to their banks. The other reason is that the perception of risk is different in that environment. Fraudsters in these economies are not keen to defraud the local populace. The reason is simple. The locals in these economies have mediocre financial power. The venom is rather turned on advanced economies that have electronic communication lines and networks that are accessible and vulnerable to risk and attack. An example is the FORTUNA ALLIANCE case mentioned in chapter 1. The different perceptions of risk dictate the priorities of fraudsters.

The implications of such vulnerability demand that risk assessment methods should have holistic and true capabilities that address risk problems from a universal perspective and context. This is completely missing from current international information security standards. The fundamental problem and flaw within present standards is that the initiators and facilitators that drive them lack an understanding of what constitutes risk in developing economies. This is analogous to the modern approach in systems development called (JAD) joint application development. This approach was advocated as a result of high incidence of failure in projects. Previous approaches to system development hardly appreciated the role of users. This development approach engages users of a system called the stakeholders by encouraging them to participate in the systems development process. A similar approach is advocated in this text in the development of international electronic security standards called the joint standards development approach (JSDA) pronounced as *jasda*. *The International community comprising members of both advanced and developing economies could develop this into acceptable standards.*

3.2.4 Implications of a non holistic approach to standards

One of the key problems to the discourse is the way developers care more about their convenience than that of the users. Sentiments shared by Odlyzko(2000). The industry has a vested interest in giving customers new products. Likewise, the customers hail developers new products on the market without comprehensive testing. This results in what I call, *premature distribution of hardware and software across the globe, hence resulting in poor global standards.* A second effect on users is what I also call *the technology vicious cycle, a form of misdirection also known in this book as the (Bandwagon syndrome).*

We could also deduce some economic sense from the French economist Julie Dupuit in 1849 who wrote the following; " *It is not because of the few thousand francs which have to be spent to put a roof over the third-class carriages or to upholster the third-class seats that some company or other has open carriages with wooden benches. What the company is trying to do is to prevent the passengers who pay the second-class fare from travelling third class; it hits the poor, not because it wants to hurt them, but to frighten the rich? And it is again for the same reason that the companies, having proven almost cruel to the third-class passengers and mean to the second class ones, become lavish in dealing with first-class passengers. Having refused the poor what is necessary, they give the rich what is superfluous."* This is interpreted to mean that the rich will always have access to better services than the poor not because services are allocated discriminately. It is because the poor has no economic power.

3.2.5 Security spending

In the paper "cyber crime outpacing security" published in the e-commerce times Enos (2000). The author explains why there is an escalation of electronic crime although there is a relative increase in security spending. The results of the survey showed that spending millions of dollars or pounds as a way of adopting security practices did not guarantee security (See table 2 in section 3.2.6). The survey also revealed that 37% of the 1,897 IT companies and information security professionals that participated in the survey reported that their company experienced a DoS (Denial of Service) attack from an attacker outside the company.

58% of the participants reported that there were persons within the company that violated access controls. 41% had destroyed or distributed confidential company information.

3.2.6 Security spending from ISCA.net Survey 2000

Table 2 – Security Spending

Sector	Estimated Average Budget($)
Consulting Firms	2,000,000
Banking and Finance Companies	950,000
High-tech Service Providers	900,000
High-tech hardware and Software manufacturers	775,000
Educational	100,000
Medical/Health	250,000

The findings indicated that the best defence against cyber crime was not spending lots of money on security systems. It rather suggested that more time was needed in thinking about appropriate security measures and solutions. Trends in security spending in recent years suggest that estimated budgets have been on the ascendancy (See table 2). Capital expenditure on equipment has not been that high. This is due to the fact that hardware and software are relatively cheaper in advanced economies. On the contrary developing economies have high estimated budgets on capital equipment, such as Software and Hardware. Risk spending is relatively low. There is *poor prioritisation of international and national funding in technological support. Fund disbursements at the company level whether in developing and advanced economies are not rationally disbursed. There is also some kind of misdirection or bandwagon effect in this case.* These factors contribute to security vulnerability. Companies and organisations sometimes seem to over estimate risk. This same bandwagon effect was also seen during the Y2K risk assessment exercise. Some countries were able to understand the risk factors better than other countries; as a result expenditure on the risk assessment exercise was not over estimated.

See Case study, analysis and evaluation of the report depicting the planning of the risk assessment exercise in section 3.2.7 & 3.2.8 Extracts from InfoDev. news release No. 99/2078/s.

3.2.7 The Case Study. World Bank (1998)

The purpose of using the World Bank's Y2K case as an example in this book is to provide the reader with a background of how risk assessment has been approached globally in recent times. It reinforces the thesis of this book which is based on the hypothesis that synchronisation of e-security between advanced and developing economies information system platforms provide richer and better security globally. This is because the case study provides an insight into how the international development association under the umbrella of the World Bank pursues policies that attempt to harmonise the economic, business and information disparities that exist within the international community. This highlights the gap between these two economic platforms.

The central analysis and evaluations made in this case are based on the levels of investments made in the risk assessment methods and exercises conducted during the Y2K project. It is a comparison between investments and estimated budget of developed and advanced countries.

Estimating costs

According to the report, estimating the costs of implementing the Y2K program was a very hard and complex exercise.

Capers Jones' hypothesis

Assuming Capers Jones' hypothesis for a global estimate of the economic impact of the Y2K Problem Jones(2000). It seems that *total cost of compliance may be up to three times that of the software repairs and correction costs*, with a very significant portion of this figure assigned to litigation costs (about 20% of the total). This hypothesis is not based on actual risk but rather on perceived risk of the future. Refer to table 3 for a detailed breakdown of costs.

38

Table 3 – Global Costs – Year 2000 Remedial Actions

Action	Global Costs (US$ billion)
Initial Software Repairs	530
Secondary "bad fix" software repairs	50
Test library Repairs	75
Data base Repairs	454
Hardware Chip Replacements	76
Hardware Performance Upgrades	150
Litigation and Damages	300
WORLD TOTAL	*1,635*

NATIONAL COORDINATING BODIES AND ACTIONS FOR REMEDIATION OF THE YEAR 2000 PROBLEMS

3.2.8 Assessment of the World Bank's report

Synchronising risk methods for e-security should be the focal point at this level. Procedures for dealing with the risk should be clearly identified and specified. The evaluation of the World Bank report shows that both advanced and developing countries as at 1998 had taken certain initiatives in conjunction with their co-ordinating national bodies as tabulated in tables 4 and 5. The case study indicates that there were four main areas of study in the planning process. These were awareness education, monitoring oversight, coordination cooperation and technical advice. Table 6 is a summary of countries and their areas of participation in the Y2K initiative.

Table 4- National Co-ordinating Bodies of OECD countries initiatives for the Y2K problem.

Country	National Co-ordinating Bodies	Targeted Sector	Main Emphases			
			Awareness Education	Monitoring Oversight	Coordination Cooperation	Technical Advice
Netherlands	National Millennium Platform	Public/Private	✔	✔	✔	✔
	Gov't Y2K Project Office	Public	✔	✔		
New-Zealand	Year 2000 Task Force	Public	✔			
Norway	Mn. of Trade & Industry	Public/ Private	✔		✔	
	Action Year 2000 Unit	Public	✔		✔	
Poland	Mn. of Interior and Administration		✔	✔		✔
	Co-ordinating Com (Telecom and IT Dept.)					
Portugal	Intersectoral Committee for IT	Public/Private	✔		✔	✔
	(supported by Mn. of Finance Informatics Institute)					
	Mn. of Science & Tech. Mission Team	Public	✔	✔	✔	✔
Spain	Ministry of Public Administrations	Public	✔	✔	✔	✔
	National Commission	Public/Private	✔		✔	
Sweden	Millennium Commission	Public/Private	✔		✔	
	Agency for Admin. Development	Public	✔		✔	
Switzerland	Jahr 2000 Ausschuss	Public/Private	✔	✔	✔	✔
United Kingdom	Year 2000 Team (Cabinet Office)	Public		✔	✔	
	Action 2000	Private	✔			
United States	President's Council on Year 2000 Conversion	Public/Private	✔		✔	

Table 5 –Extracts of Y2K initiatives of some developing countries

Country	Y2K body	Overseeing body	Awareness Education	Monitoring	Coordination Cooperation	Technical Advice
AFRICA						
Burkina Faso	Délégation Générale Informatique	Cabinet du Premier Ministre	√			√
Cameroon	Comité An 2000	**Ministry of Public Investments and regional development -** General Secretary	√	√	√	√
Eritrea	National Committee for Y2K	Eritrean Information Systems Agency	√	√	√	√
Mauritania	Not Available	Ministère des Finances - Direction de l'Informatique	√	√	√	√
Namibia	Not Available	Office of the Prime Minister - Department of Administration and Information Technology Management	√	√	√	√
Rwanda	Not Available	Office of the Vice-President - Direction of Computer Services	√		√	√
Senegal	Not Available	Ministere de la Recherche Scientifique et de la Technologie - Délégation a l'informatique	√	√	√	√
South Africa	National Year 2000 Decision Support Center	Ministry of Post, Telecommunications & Broadcasting	√	√	√	√

*Source: info*Dev Developing Countries database.

Table 6 – Advanced countries participation

Sectors	Advanced Countries		Developing Countries	
	Number of Countries	Percentage of participation %	Number of Countries	Percentage of participation
Awareness education	25	92	22	95.9
Monitoring	14	51	17	78.3
Co-ordination and co-operation	19	70	19	82.6
Technical advice	13	49	20	86.2

A breakdown analysis of table 6 indicates that the rate of participation in the four areas among developing countries was higher than participation in advanced countries in all sectors as at that time.

Table 7 indicates a higher percentage of participation in the four sectors amongst developing economies.

Table 7 – Ratio analysis of developing to advance countries

Sector	Percentage of participation of African countries in relation to advanced countries
Awareness education	3.9% higher
Monitoring	27.3% higher
Co-ordination and co-operation	12.6% higher
Technical advice	37.2% higher

The varying levels of participation as highlighted in table 4 and 5 could be explained by the fact that developing economies generally do not see the difference between actual risk and perceived risk. In most cases actual risk is taken as perceived risk. It is important to understand that perceived risk is only possible when there are standards. In the Western world people lock their doors both day and night because there are perceived risks, this is a de facto standard. On the contrary most people in developing economies especially in Africa will not care locking their doors in broad day light. This is because there are no perceived risks. Children could also play at any radius without parents perceiving risk, because there is no fear of abduction.

Another classical case is the seat belt legislation that was passed in at least 80 Jurisdictions across the world in 1991. Studies conducted by (GM) General Motors showed that it was only in the United Kingdom that fatalities results were recorded Adams (1999). Majority of the countries involved in the studies did not see the significant impact of the introduction of seat belts. These examples depict that standards whether being de facto or initiated through government policy can not be applied unilaterally. This is shown from the findings of the empirical studies in this chapter. Perceived risk normally comes from awareness. The above analysis of the World Bank report highlights that almost 96% of developing countries needed an awareness programme as indicated in table 6. A similar percentage was on technical advice.

Although some developing countries could perceive risk, there are economic issues why the perceived risk is not highly prioritised. Computer machinery in developing economies is implemented to sustain mainly operational activities rather than strategic ones. Funding of such projects goes into initial capital and equipment funding. Routine risk assessment exercises to maintain the continuous performance of these systems is lowly prioritised thereby affecting the adherence to best practices. This is what is meant by, *Poor prioritisation of international and national funding in technologies that support developing economies.*

Table 8 – Risk spending on Y2K project on selected OECD countries

Countries	Contributions to National Assessment exercise	Contributions to OECD	Contributions to international community
UK	$26.7m	$25,000	$16.7m
Canada	-		
Netherlands	$6.5m	-	-
Australia			-
Belgium	$4.4-	-	-
France	$7.1	-	-
Ireland	-	-	-
Mexico		-	-
Norway	$11.o	-	-
Japan	$7	-	-
Finland	$17	-	-
Denmark		-	-
Sweden		-	-
Spain		-	-
Switzerland	$13	-	-

There were no significant contributions made to countries within neighbourhood regions. This was the information available at consulates and respective ministries and government department (See table 9).

44

Table 9 **Risk spending on Y2K project on selected developing countries**

Countries	Contributions to National Assessment exercise	Contributions to regional countries	Contributions to international community
Burkina Faso	-	-	-
Cameroon	$-1m	-	-
Eritrea	-	-	-
Mauritania	-	-	-
Namibia	-	-	-
Rwanda	-	-	-
Senegal	-	-	-
South Africa	$7m-	-	-
Uganda	--	-	-
Croatia	-	-	-
Romania	-	-	-
Brazil	-	-	-
Chile	-	-	-
Colombia	-	-	-
Jamaica	-	-	-

Below are the seven main factors that could have contributed to such disparity of levels of participation. These factors are explained as elements of proof and reasons from empirical studies as to why there is a gap between technologies that support developing economies and the advanced world. It shows that risk assessment spending is far higher than risk mitigation and prevention technology spending.

- *Lack of integration in preventive technologies,*
- *Mal preference in global technology schemes*
- *Poor prioritization of international and national funding in technologies that support developing and advanced economies*
- *Premature distribution of hardware and software across the globe (Poor global standards)*
- *Mal certification of software and hardware (lack of certification bodies in developing economies*
- *Disparities in human ware that support technologies across the globe*
- *Technology vicious cycle, this is what I call misdirection (Bandwagon syndrome)*

These are the seven factors in this study identified as elements that have caused the gap in technological risk between developing and advanced economies. For any information systems security risk analyst to get it right, the technological gap needs to be harmonised by synchronisation. Although the desired objective would have been closing the gap, it is not quite possible in the short and medium term. In the short and medium term we need a harmony between the advanced economies information systems security platforms and the systems of developing world. These seven factors are assessed through the framework of the empirical studies and a method of synchronisation outlined in the toolkit in chapter 5.

3.3 Policies and Standards

Government policies and standards designed to direct the global economic information era must be critically evaluated and reviewed. Until recently customers had to queue at counters in order to withdraw money, cash their cheques and transfer funds. Today the use of sophisticated technology in the banking sector has enabled us to enjoy direct banking service in the comfort of our homes. This has been made possible as a result of e-government policies Gonzi (2001). It is important for us to bear in mind that information security management as an issue, is an international one. This point is stressed here because the investigations conducted indicate that, inasmuch as most governments are keen in getting the problem improved there is basically a drive towards policies and standards that are being developed only in specific countries, without much attention given to other nations. It is the writer's opinion and belief that what is needed is a joint international consultation platform with reference to what kind of policies and standards which when implemented will achieve international consensus. International consensus means international security support. What it actually implies is that policies and standards, covering information security, must not be derived by only the giants in technology, such as Japan, America or UK.

Let us briefly examine a debate that took place on the 22nd October 1997 at the House of Lords. Lord Renwick, former Chairman of the IMIS (Institute for the Management of Information Systems) political advisory committee, opened a short debate on electronic commerce asking her Majesty's government "What steps they intended to take to ensure the city of London remains the leading centre for world-wide electronic trade in the face of United States government initiatives intended to ensure that internet-based commerce is conducted under US security standards" Campbell (1997)?

In the introductory analysis it was mentioned that national policies and standards derived and proposed as international standards and policies were unlikely to work in the long term. How could one or two countries solve an issue that needs global participation and co-operation? The open remarks by Lord Renwick during the debate on such an issue of global concern defeated the purpose it was intended to achieve. Although Lord Renwick set the "ball rolling" by asking such a provocative and thought challenging question, the end result of such a debate was to determine policies and standards, which were to be formulated to guide the future of information security management in the UK.

Recapturing the introduction of the debate, quoting Lord Renwick, he said *"We hear much talk of the global information society of the future and appear to assume that the language will be American, the cultural values those of Hollywood and the legal values of Perry Mason."*

It is not clear what these remarks meant, whether he made them because America had taken the initiative to set standards and policies which were supposedly going to govern the security management of electronic trade world wide, without UK taking the lead in policies and standards or he had the rest of the world in mind. If the presumption made here is right, then he equally advocated and supported the notion in the debate that setting of policies and standards must be approached on an international platform. Although approaching the setting of policies and standards from the basis and perception of leaders in the development of the technology is not completely wrong, such a regional approach must only be designed by all interest groups world wide and subsequently submitted to an international forum for discussion.

Adopting a guideline such as (BS7799) British standards 7799 is a way of ensuring that the required standards are upheld. This ensures that security breaches are prevented. This is because it has already earned international recognition and acceptance as a very productive way forward to ensuring information systems process certification. Organisations can have their implementation of the BS7799 evaluated and certified under any accredited certification scheme Ellof.,Solms(2002).

3.3.1 Shortfalls of current policies and standards

The problem with all these standards spearheaded by advanced economies stem from the fact that *developing economies are not empowered in the design of international policies that ultimately become the driving force and bedrock of international standards in information security. Developing economies rather adopt international security standards that are already packaged.*

It is no doubt why most of these economies do not see the relevance of such standards. This assertion and notion can not also be understated, since it is even strengthened by the statement made by a republican presidential candidate of the USA, George Bush in response to questions regarding foreign policy to Africa in a pre-election interview in 2001. He stated "Africa does not matter". This statement might have several connotations. I interpret this *as* "Africa is at the bottom of his scale of preference and priorities". Probably this might be the finest and polished way of presenting it. His post enthronement agenda was quite on the contrary. At least he embarked upon a five day tour of Africa to put his critics to shame. The speculation and interpretation to this voyage is that September 11 2001 might have changed his view about national and global security. Quoting the president of the World Bank in response to a television interview on BBC1 via a video link post September 11 2001, "It *is important for us in this part of the globe with economic power to realise that there are no walls protecting us"*. His statement stressed on the importance of global security. Rise or fall together. This seems to be the first move to understanding global issues that affect all mankind. The Internet through its web has intertwined all nations. This has resulted in a lot of problems, including *Mal certification of software and hardware (lack of certification bodies in developing economies)* which has increased electronic risk across the globe.

3.3.2 Efforts by developing economies

Currently there are some efforts being made by some professionals in developing economies to ensure that there are standards that govern and regulate the use of the Internet. An example is in South Africa where a group ensuring excellent practice have been formed. This group is called, the (ISPA) Internet Service Providers Association of South Africa. The association brings together approximately 63 ISPs.

Below are extracts from the association's code of practice.

- Freedom of expression
- Privacy and confidentiality

48

- Consumer protection and provision of information to customers
- Unsolicited bulk mail
- Cyber crime
- Protection of minors
- Unlawful content activity
- Internet Standards

The association also states that ISPA members will operate in accordance with established Internet best practices, as set out in the various (RFC) request for documents and as mandated from time to time by established and requested Internet governance structures. This is commendable at the national level regarding practicing standards. However investigations conducted among the ISPs in South Africa revealed that their service standards differed. Example, according to information gathered from their websites, large companies such as DataPro Ltd and Infosat Ltd, security services covered security audits for clients, whiles security services for AT & T Global Networks and Connect IT-NetraLink did not explicitly state that as part of the security services they provided.

The implications of this inconsistency could be risky. This is because it opens up avenues for areas that are vulnerable to attacks. The findings from the empirical evaluations detail the security gaps that exist from poor standardisation and certification of computer products among the rest of the developing economies.

Having considered policies and standards derived by governments to ensure international security, I consider aspects of technical standards that, if not adhered to might infringe security, thus product certification.

3.3.3 Product certification

This is one way of ensuring security in systems. However certification must be one that could be trusted. So government sponsored certification is preferable. There are two leaders in this area, TCSEC (Trusted Computer Systems Evaluation Criteria) in the USA and ITSEC (Information Technology Security Evaluation and Certification) in Europe. Both the US and Europe are trying to develop reciprocity in certification in the form of 'Common Criteria' but there are serious problems with the concept of common criteria Townsend (1997). This implies that all security products that are to be brought to the information technology market must be subjected to certification. Unfortunately that is not the case. Most products that come to the market bypass certification. Although there are no tough regulations pertaining to this, the author believes it is the responsibility of government certification groups to create awareness in the banking industry to verify whether all systems implemented have passed certification tests. If a particular security system has not gone through certification, then it will be appropriate for potential customers to reject that product. By customers doing that, they help the schemes set up for security standards to work effectively. TCSEC is commonly known as the orange book standards, originally published in 1985. The C2 classification in the orange book is best known probably because it is most likely to be relevant to personal computers. It is however important to note that C2 is described as "The recommended minimum security standards" Townsend (1997).

3.3.4 A hypothetical case of certification

Now let us look at a case against certification. A hypothetical application that seeks to provide security for Windows XP. Although the Window XP is a very popular operating system with enhanced security features, it is still insecure. Let us make the assumption that there is such an attractive product that achieves C2 certification. If that assumption is correct then, the first argument is that accepting security certification as a rubber stamp may not be exactly what it seems. The other areas that might elude bankers will be when a particular product passes certification. This might make them presume that the product is safe and as a result may not take into consideration other security procedures which are not implemented. For instance, Physical security of the equipment and administrative security procedures might be overlooked. In view of this misnomer of certification, it is said that for a product to meet the minimum standards of certification, it must protect the confidentiality, integrity and availability of data. It is also thought that the major problem with these certification schemes is that, most were developed or designed based on military mind set. Confidentiality comes first; the commercial world usually considers confidentiality as less important to integrity. *Mal certification of software and hardware due to the lack of certification bodies in developing economies* has increased electronic risk across the globe. This is seen in a more analytical detail from studies conducted on the field in chapter 4.

3.3.5 Summary of chapter 3

This chapter was an examination and dialogue of risk assessment methods, policies and standards that supported e-security. It highlighted the processes and stages involved in implementing ISMS and risk management systems.

The stages were as follows:

- Purchasing of security standards
- Training personnel of the client to implement security standard
- Assembling of a team and agreeing on a strategy
- Making an assessment of the risk
- Designing a document that outlines the policies of the system and choosing a registrar to certify the system

The economics of security was also discussed with emphasis on equilibrium of economies, and how economies affected risk and fraud.
Risk spending was discussed using the World Bank's Y2K assessment exercise as a case study. The appropriate implementation of Policies, Standards and Certification procedures were also investigated.

Chapter 4

Empirical analysis and evaluations of Case studies

An empirical evaluation is the appraisal of a theory by observation in experiments based on a field study. This study is an assessment of the elements of proof of the notion that the key to excellent global security is by synchronising the technological gap between advanced and developing economies and that risk assessment spending should not be higher than risk mitigation and prevention technology spending.

The factors that have been identified and tested as the fundamental cause of the gap in technologies and security methods affecting risk management are summarised as follows and also highlighted in sections 3.2.8 of chapter 3 as part of discussions on risk assessment:

- *Lack of integration in preventive technologies*
- *Mal preference in global technology schemes*
- *Poor prioritisation of national and international funding in technologies that support developing and advanced economies*
- *Premature distribution of hardware and software across the globe NAP (1990)*
- *Mal certification of software and hardware*
- *Disparities in human ware that support technologies across the globe*
- *Technology vicious cycle, this is what I call misdirection (Bandwagon syndrome).*

These factors were highlighted in previous chapters as part of central points of discussions.

4.1 Methodology

This study commences by looking at the technological infrastructure of selected countries in advanced and developing economies. An assessment of the results gathered from the ISPs that participated in the study is carried out. The emphasis is on communications, thus Telephone, Mobile and the Internet. The background information provided in relation to the communications infrastructure was extracted from the annual report of the world fact book 2002 of the CIA (central intelligence agency). This source was then critically evaluated with current field data. Conclusions have been drawn from the entire evaluations.

4.2 Assessment of Communication Technologies by continent

4.2.1 List of essential global communication technologies

- (MMR/MRRL) Micro Radio Relay Link

A Transmission line capable of sending long distance telephone calls and television programs by highly directional radio microwaves. These microwaves are received and sent from one booster station to another on an optical path.

- (WLL) Wireless Local Loop

Wireless radio based transmission that has high frequencies.

- (CC) Coaxial Cable

A multi channel communication cable consisting of a central conducting wire, surrounded by and insulated from a cylindrical conducting shell; a large number of telephone channels can be made available within the insulated space by the use of a large number of carrier frequencies.

- (SC)Submarine Cable

A cable designed for the transmission of data under water.

- (MC)Mobile Cellular

Mobile communication device that has transmitter and receiver that could communicate globally.

- (FO)Fibre Optic

A multi-channel communications cable using a thread of optical glass fibres as a transmission medium in which the signal (voice, video, etc.) is in the form of a coded pulse of light.

- (DMRR) Digital Microwave Radio Relay

A Transmission line capable of sending long distance telephone calls and television programs by highly directional radio microwaves. These microwaves are received and sent from one booster station to another on a digital path via modems.

- SCS (INTELSAT)

A communication system consisting of two or more earth stations and at least one satellite that provide long distance transmission of voice, data, and television; the system usually serves as a trunk connection between telephone exchanges; if the earth stations are in the same country, it is a domestic system. (INTELSAT) International Satellite Organisation

- SES (Satellite earth station)

A Communication system that has a microwave radio transmitting and receiving antenna that is capable of communicating with satellites.

The communication technologies listed in section 4.2.1 are essential technologies that enable people, organisations and countries to communicate across the globe. These technologies possess sophisticated features that support effective communication systems. Table 10 shows the types of the listed technologies available to both developing and advanced countries.

4.2.2 *Communication ability of countries in continental regions across the world*

Table 10 shows that countries across the world whether based in advanced or developing economies have the ability to communicate both in continental regions and the world as a whole.

The essential technologies listed in section 4.2.1 are available and accessible by both developing and advanced economies. For example the numbers of *Intelsat* within the reach of some developing countries are equal to that of some advanced countries (See table 10). This denotes that countries across the world have the capability to communicate whether economically rich or poor. Notwithstanding this state of global communication capabilities, the standards that govern the application of technologies between the two types of economies are far from being equal. Secondly investments in risk prevention and mitigation technologies are not balanced. This situation as highlighted earlier on becomes one of the central sources of global risk. The problem of *poor prioritisation of national and international funding in technologies that supports developing economies* highlighted throughout this literature should be addressed by reversing the trend of fund disbursements.

Economic power for instance has an effect on technology accessibility. This means that people within strong economies have more contact to information and communication technology than people within weak economies. For example it is estimated that 1% of people in Ghana have access to the Internet, whilst in the USA it is estimated that 50% of the people have access to the Internet. In Sweden almost 90% of people have access to the Internet (See table 11), this is a reflection of economic strength. Although there are significant differences in the number of people who have access to the Internet, the importance of Internet accessibility and availability should not be based on numbers or quantities. It should rather be based on qualitatively analysis. This is because risk is a qualitative issue and not a quantitative one. We may attempt to allocate values to risk. The relativity of risk makes the allocation of values to risk a highly unlikely prediction of actual risk. For example Internet banking is done in both developing and advanced economies. Barclays Bank provides Internet Banking facilities in both advanced and developing countries. Risk in Internet Banking with Barclays Bank could lie within the framework of the ISP of any country. The remote connection to Barclays servers assuming managed by Dell Computers should be routed via telephone lines of the country where the service is being sought. Risk vulnerability will be dependent on the quality of security supporting communication lines. This implies that the level of risk will depend on whether users could sniff information packets, conduct effective traffic analysis or use some kind of brute force to obtain information during Internet banking transactions. The bottom line is that both advanced and developing economies have the capability to communicate using modern technologies. It is on these grounds that the synchronisation of security methods becomes paramount.

Table 10 shows data on countries and technologies that support communications Infrastructure

Country	MRR	MRRL	WLL	CC	SES	SC	MC	FO	DMRR	NO. OF ITELSAT
AFRICA										
Ghana	√	√	√	√	√	√	√	√	√	4
Nigeria	√	√		√	√	√	√			3
Senegal	√			√	√	√		√		1
South Africa	√	√	√	√	√	√	√	√	√	3
ASIA										
China				√	√	√	√	√		5
Japan	√	√	√	√	√	√	√	√	√	5
India	√			√	√	√	√	√		8
Pak.	√			√	√	√	√	√	√	3
Sri Lanka	√			√	√	√	√	√	√	2
Singapore	√	√	√	√	√	√	√	√	√	2
EU.										
UK	√	√	√	√	√	√	√	√	√	10
France	√	√	√	√	√	√	√	√	√	2
Germany.	√	√	√	√	√	√	√	√	√	N/A
Sweden	√	√	√	√	√	√	√	√	√	1
AMERICAS.										
USA	√	√	√	√	√	√	√	√	√	61
Canada	√	√	√	√	√	√	√	√	√	5
MIDDLE EAST										
Iran	√	√		√	√	√	√	√		9
Israel	√	√	√		√	√	√	√	√	3
Saudi Arabia	√	√	√	√	√	√	√	√	√	5

4.2.3 Communications Infrastructure across the World

The purpose of the information in table 11 is to provide the reader with the background of the technological infrastructure, thus telecommunications capabilities available to IT companies (Internet Service Providers) that serve people and organisations in the countries listed for this study. It highlights the fact that both developing and advanced economies communicate and share information using the Internet. It also highlights the importance of taking stock or inventory of the technological capabilities of countries across the globe whether rich or poor as amplified in this example by the CIA of the United States of America. If there is anything that has brought developing economies and countries closer to advanced nations, in terms of information power then it is the Internet. This assertion has also been discussed by Shapiro and Varian (1998) in their book "information rules". The authors points out that although there have been changes in technology, economic laws have not changed. Demand for information somehow is inelastic. There is a form of interdependency in the world of network connectivity in the application and utilisation of information and communication technologies. Information is also available so quickly and so inexpensively due to the ubiquitous nature of the Internet.

4.2.4 Ratio analysis of ISPs versus Internet Users

Ratio analysis of ISPs to Internet Users from table 11 shows that both advanced and developing economies have similar level of distribution when it comes to the number of users to an ISP. This analysis could have several interpretations. The general interpretation given in this work is that numbers of persons that receive Internet services from individual ISPs in both advanced and developing economies fall within similar ranges. For example ISPs in Senegal support on average 100,000 people. A similar number is supported by ISPs in United Kingdom which is 85,000. It should be realised that it is not the subject of this book to discuss issues related to capacity and performance. The dimensions between capacity and service users are mainly due to the quality, effectiveness, reliability and efficiency of the services provided by the ISPs in respective countries.

Table 11 shows data on countries, number of main line telephones, Number of mobile cellular, Internet Service Providers, Internet Users and Populations.

Country	Population	Number of Main lines	No of Mobile Cellular	Internet Service Providers	Internet Users
AFRICA					
Ghana	20,244,154	240,000	150,000	12 @ year 2000	200,000
Nigeria	129,934,911	500,000	200,000	11 @ year 2000	100,000
Senegal	10,589,571	234,916	373,965	1 @ year 2000	100,000
South Africa	43,647,658	5m	7.06m	150 @ year 2001	3.068m
ASIA					
China	1,284,303,705	135m	65m	3 @ year 2000	45.8m
Japan	126,974,628	60.381m	63.88m	73 @ year 2000	56m
India	1,045,845,226	27.7m	2.93m	43 @ year 2000	7m
Pakistan	147,663,429	2.861m	158,000	30 @ year 2000	1.2m
Sri Lanka	19,576,783	494,509	228,604	5 @ year 2000	121,500
Singapore	4,452,732	1.95m	2.74m	9 year @ 2000	2.31m
EUROPE					
United Kingdom	59,778,002	34.878m	43.5m	400 @ year 2000	34.3m
France	59,765,983	34.86m	11.078m	62 @ 2000	16.97m
Germany	83,251,851	50.9m	55.3m	200 @ 2000	32.1m
Sweden	8,876,744	6.017m	3.835m	29 @ 2000	6.02
AMERICAS					
United States of America	280,562,849	194m	69m	7000 @ year 2002	165.75m
Canada	31,902,268	20,802,900 m	8.76m	760@2000	16.84m
MIDDLE EAST					
Iran	66,622,704	6.313 m	265,000	8 @ year 2000	420,000
Israel	6,029,529	2.8m	2.5m	21 @ year 2000	1.94m
Saudi Arabia	23,513,330	3.1m	1m	42 @ year 2001	570,000

4.2.5 Analysis of results amongst ISPs and Service Subscribers on the field

Seventeen Companies comprising ISPs and Service Subscribers contributed directly whilst seven companies made indirect contributions via providing guidance to sources of relevant information to this study. Contributions were also made by a few consulates representing certain countries in developing economies. Responses in tables 12 to 14 represent the practices and framework upon which these companies made contributions to in appendix 1. Most of the field studies focused on data from developing economies, since relevant data from advanced economies were available from sources such as (Forrester.com). Table 12 is analysis of investments on risk preventive technologies in developing and advanced economies.

Table 12 - Investments on risk prevention technologies

AMOUNT ($)	Number of Companies in advanced economies	Number of Companies in developing economies
None	-	-
1000- 5000	-	7
5000 – 10000	2	3
Above 10,000	9	1

Table 12 shows that out of the 22 companies that responded to the test, none of the companies in advanced economies invested less than $5000. 9 companies invested more than $10,000. This pattern in risk investment also reflected in some aspects of the literature.

Table 13 shows investments in risk assessment exercises. The results of the responses show that investments in risk assessment exercises amongst companies in advanced economies exceeded that of developing economies. 9 of the companies in advanced economies said that investment went above $10,000. 2 of the companies' investment in risk assessment exercises fell between $ 5000 and $10,000.

Table 13 - Investments on risk assessment exercises

AMOUNT ($)	Number of Companies in advanced economies	Number of Companies in developing economies
None	-	8
1000- 5000	-	1
5000 – 10000	1	1
Above 10,000	11	2

- Risk assessment methods adopted by developing economies Companies

14 Companies were tested in assessment methods. 10 of these companies were not able to specify any type of risk assessment method used.
The remaining 4 companies seemed to be more comfortable with British Standards (BS779). There were no plans for risk assessment exercises. This was more prominent amongst ISPs in the region. On the contrary companies in advanced economies had routine risk assessment exercises. The frequency of risk assessment exercises amongst companies in developing economies was lower, compared to companies in advanced economies.

Table 14 depict different expertise types amongst manpower of developing and advanced economies. There were 11 companies from advanced economies and 13 companies from developing economies who participated in the test. Most of the companies from advanced economies at least had two of the expertise types listed in table 14.

Table 14 – Security Expertise

	Netware	Unix/Linux	Windows	Cisco Technology
Companies in advanced economies	8	10	11	10
Companies in developing economies	3	7	7	8

Tables 14 shows that the manpower in both advanced and developing economies had similar security skills. The level of expertise in each of these areas was not verified in detail, since there was no immediate criterion in measuring experience in using those skills.

4.3 Discussions on empirical studies

- **Reasons why synchronisation of e-security methods is vital**

4.3.1 Technologies that support electronic transactions are globally available to both advanced and developing economies (see table 10 and 11).

The global economy has technologies, which are available and accessible by both developing and advanced economies. There are also electronic commerce activities in both types of economies. The current technological age makes risk assessment of security in a global context a critical programme. Tables 10 and 11 for instance show that there are active Internet Users across the globe regardless of economic strength. Although the percentage of user participation of the Internet is not similar everywhere across the globe, there is evidence that developing economies have technologies that enable them to engage in electronic transactions similar to that of advanced economies. The author thinks that when it comes to the application of technology, mass or size does not matter much. A small mass of a certain type of technology can depict vulnerability that could be used as a means of harmful attack.

4.3.2 The weaknesses in security that exist in electronic fund transfer, Internet and Telephone Banking could be exploited by electronic criminals across the globe.

This suggests that it is important to synchronise the communications infrastructure available to both developing and advanced economies. It has been advocated strongly in this text that synchronising security among economies is critical. The lack of synchronisation of these security platforms leaves a security gap. Hackers and intruders could exploit the gaps in security. The present gap can be harmonised by encouraging the appropriate standards and policies as discussed in chapters 2 and 3. The policies and standards should fit the economic structure of developing economies. It has been highlighted in chapter 3 that risk is relative and subjective. The risks associated with technologies in advanced economies are not the same as those in developing economies. These are important factors that every risk analyst, systems manager and information systems management consultant should be aware of.

4.3.3 Risk assessment of authentication methods needs to be improved due to the lack of holistic approach in the design of security policies and standards. Certification processes in advanced economies do not integrate risks that evolve from developing economies.

The rules that constitute the design of security policies and algorithms do not integrate risk factors that evolve from developing economies. This means those security software designs do not anticipate risks and vulnerability that might evolve from the Internet platforms of developing economies (See models in Chapter 5). It is time for designers and developers to investigate risk factors that might cause harm as a result of such weaknesses. Supposing we assume that the mindsets and profiles of electronic criminals are the same, it could be argued that, electronic crime in advanced economies are similar to ones in developing economies. Perhaps that is the rationale behind the design of existing security systems and methods. Although that might be true in some instances, the platforms and means of access to vulnerable elements of communication technologies are very different as evidenced by empirical studies. This means that the avenues of attack as a result of present risk related to the communication technologies of developing economies are more compared to that of advanced economies.

4.3.4 E-trade is on the ascendancy in both developing and advanced economies. This drives the need to employ security methods based on standards that reflect the current state of technology globally.

Current global electronic business trends show that e-trade is still on the rise although there have been instances of Dot Com failures. There is enthusiastic participation from developing economies. The arms of central governments, banks and private companies are being encouraged to take opportunity of the competitive advantage that comes with the participation in such ventures. In advanced economies at least 60 to 70% of the population participate in some form of Tele-banking or Internet banking. Customers check their current account balances via telephone or Internet. Similar percentages of people use their credit cards to purchase items on the Internet. All these activities form part of e-trading.

4.3.5 The synchronisation of e-security methods will loosen the chains of E-trade regulations in advanced economies and make it friendlier to developing economies.

Although regulations governing trade in advanced economies are not mandatory, it suggests that there are risk factors, which could only be borne by companies who choose to violate these regulations. E-trading will continue as technology becomes more sophisticated. For instance there are new mobile communication technologies that currently work in conjunction with the Internet using protocols such as (WAP) Wireless Application Protocol Keen.,Mackintosh, (2001). These communication devices could be employed to outpace current risk prevention technologies. For instance mobile communication devices could be disabled at street market places and transferred to any part of the world. The software for carrying this task is readily available at street markets. Replacing electronic chips in these mobile devices with custom built electronic chips could be highly dangerous and risky to electronic security.

4.3.6 The human ware for both technical and non technical manpower leaves much to be desired.

The regional imbalance between developing and advanced economies needs to be addressed by channelling standards through organised bodies and structures such as governmental agencies, leading IT firms in these economies and interested academics. This could be achieved by both advanced and developing economies taking initiatives, which will be embraced by both economic communities. Such initiatives could be achieved through international conferences and forums with the participation of governments.

4.3.7 The escalation of global electronic risk

It is also likely that risk will increase due to a relative increase in capital expenditure in communication technologies in developing economies. The pace at which technologies are permanently distributed across the globe needs to be investigated and addressed with urgency. Lack of similar pace in the advancement of standards in information security management will cause a relative increase in security spending in advanced economies. The alternative means of solving the e-trade ban and regulations is by closing the gap in risk between advanced and developing economies.

4.3.8 Findings from empirical studies (See section 4.2.5) depict that developing economies have placed less importance on risk spending. Although there are existing risks from the gap analysis conducted, there is still an increase in capital expenditure rather than risk mitigation technologies. The contrast shows that advanced economies over estimate risk.

Each of the steps discussed above will go a long way to help developing economies gain the credibility necessary for e-trading which will eventually reduced risk globally. It may also increase investment drive in developing economies in the medium term. This will ultimately have an effect on global economic productivity.

A toolkit has been proposed for synchronising e-security methods in global electronic transactions in Chapter 5.

4.4 Summary of chapter 4

Chapter 4 was an assessment of findings from empirical studies. There was an examination of communications infrastructure across the globe. Emphasis was placed on the services provided by ISPs. There were discussions on the importance of e-synchronisation. The discussions on the vitality of e-synchronisation centred on technologies that supported electronic transactions globally, risk associated with such technologies and its' impact on e-trade. Weaknesses in security that existed in the framework of electronic fund transfer, Internet and Telephone banking were highlighted as weaknesses that could be exploited by electronic criminals. The lack of a holistic approach to authentication highlighted the need for improvements via synchronisation. It was discussed that the rules that constituted the design of security policies and algorithms did not integrate risk factors that evolved from operating systems platforms of developing economies. It was also discussed that e-trade was on the ascendancy in both developing and advanced economies although there were instances of Dot Com failures. Synchronisation of e-security methods was vital in loosening the chains of e-trade regulations in advanced economies. It was also seen as a means of making e-trade friendlier to developing economies. The human ware for both technical and non-technical manpower left much to be desired in both developing and advanced economies. The assessment also revealed that there was an escalation of risk.

Chapter 5

Toolkit for synchronising e-security methods in global electronic transactions

5.1 Proposed guidelines

The proposed guidelines comprise seven stages. These are as follows:

- **Integrate risk preventive technologies**

  This means that current technologies available for risk prevention should be available to both advanced and developing economies. The design aspects should also integrate features that foresee risk from a global perspective. Software designed for risk prevention should have the capability to analyse risk factors in developing economies. Adopt a context based approach to risk integration (See figure 6).

- **Prioritise global technology scheme**

  Developing of new technologies should be based on schemes that address the fundamental constraints of risk preventive technologies. For instance examine whether training schemes that support technology take a holistic approach.

- **Prioritise national and international funding in technologies that support developing and advanced economies as part of an evaluation process**

  Funding that support any form of technological development should be properly prioritised. The scale of preference of such prioritisation should be based on an understanding of the risk requirements in specific economies. This should be a context-based approach.

- **Verify premature distribution of hardware and software across the globe**

Manufacturing and Distribution of hardware and software should not be executed prematurely. Vendors of hardware and software should verify whether products being marketed meet minimum security requirements such as the C2 classification of the orange books. The buyers of these technologies should revalidate and reassess whether the products being sold to them meet security requirements that are globally acceptable. A thorough examination of security features should be beta tested by the user.

- **Ensure that certification of software and hardware is satisfactory**

Certification should be context based. It should address and predict uncertainties that might evolve in different environments. Verify the integrity of the certifier.

- **Reconcile the disparities in skills of human ware within the environment the technology will be implemented.**

Train technical and non technical manpower that interact or communicate with the technology.

- **Refuse to be misdirected by the "Bandwagon syndrome".**

Do not be led. Take the lead in the introduction of any technology or system. Before an introduction of new technology in your environment, considered assessment should be made.

The guidelines are mapped onto a set of models that form the methodology applied by the toolkit in synchronising e-security (See Figures 3 to 7)

5.2 Descriptions of Models

This section is a description of set of service server transmission models that form an integral part of the Synchronising E-Security Methodology. There are six levels in the implementation process of the Methodology. They are the following:

Level 1 of the service server transmission model is the first step in the e-synchronisation process. Identifying the risk from risk access spots is the approach adopted by this methodology. Risk spots in italics might not necessarily be risk access spots in every environment although the view taken by this book has been derived from findings of field studies. This might vary from one environment to the other. It is however recommended that these risk access spots are used as a basic guide when accessing risk spots in any Telebanking application environment. (See figure 3)

Level 2 of the service server transmission model is the second step in the e-synchronisation process. After identifying a possible risk in the application environment, the risk identified should be extracted and well documented. (See figure 4). The objective of this level is to build a trail of perceived risk in the application environment, thus banking.

Level 3 is a (RIG) Risk Identification Grid extracted from **levels 1 and 2**. The grid shows recommended Risk Access Spots on a network. The RIG was based on risk spots common to both developing and advanced economies operating and networks platforms identified in the empirical studies. See section 5.4 for definition and discussions on [1]Risk Access Spots

Level 4 is the integration of the risk. The process of identifying common and uncommon risk across all network platforms. This step is critical to the success of the synchronisation process. (See figure 5).

Level 5 is the process of auditing the risk. This stage subjects the risks to an assessment in order to determine whether the risk is perceived or actual. (See Figure 6)

- [1] **Risk Access Spots are risk points on a network which are vulnerable to attack**

NB: Areas in italic and bullet points are known as (RAS) *See Risk Access Spots of figures 3 to 7*

Level 6 is a (RISG) Risk Identification and Solution Grid. This grid shows recommended risk access spots on a network with suggested solutions from a software simulator. The RISG is based on recommended solutions provided by a security expert or the simulator which will be constructed as an integral part of the proposed toolkit.

5.3 Synchronising E-security Methodology using (SSTM) Service Server Transmission Models

Figure 3
**SYNCHRONISING E-SECURITY METHODOLOGY
USING (SSTM) SERVICE SERVER TRANSMISSION MODEL LEVEL 1**

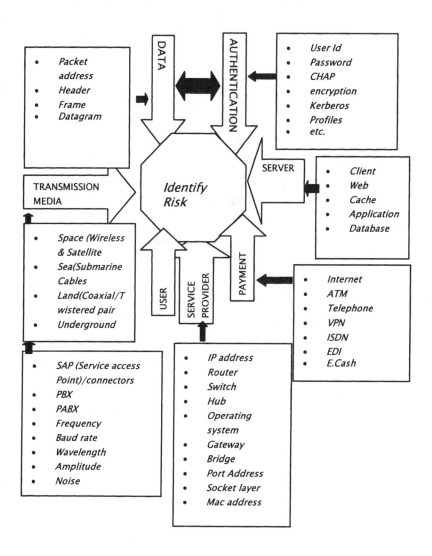

Figure 4
**SYNCHRONISING E-SECURITY METHODOLOGY
USING (SSTM) SERVICE SERVER TRANSMISSION MODEL LEVEL 2**

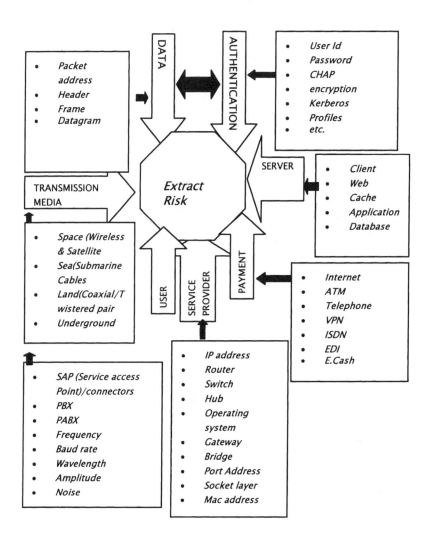

Figure 5

(RIG) Risk Identification Grid Level 3

	Z1	Z2	Z3	Z4	Z5	Z6	Z7
Z1	Skill	Location	Hub	Switch	Baudrate	Bandwith	IP-Address
Z2	Satellite	VPN	EDI	E-cash	ATM	Packet address	Router
Z3	Gateway	Terminator	E-Chip	OSS	VPN	Earth station	Wavelength
Z4	Repeater	Socket layer	Password	Cyphertext	PBX	SAP	USER ID/PIN
Z5	Frame	Connectors	Cable/Wire	Profile	Application	Amplitude	Sec. Provider
Z6	Router	Frequency	Cache Server	Dbase Server	Web Server	ISP	Noise
Z7	Client Server	SAP (Service Access Provider)	Port address	MAC address	Datagram	Protocol	Circuit

Figure 6
SYNCHRONISING E-SECURITY METHODOLOGY
USING (SSTM) SERVICE SERVER TRANSMISSION MODEL LEVEL 4

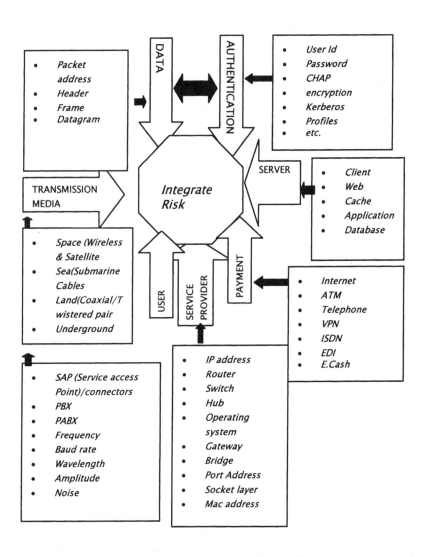

Figure 7
**SYNCHRONISING E-SECURITY METHODOLOGY
USING (SSTM) SERVICE SERVER TRANSMISSION MODEL LEVEL 5**

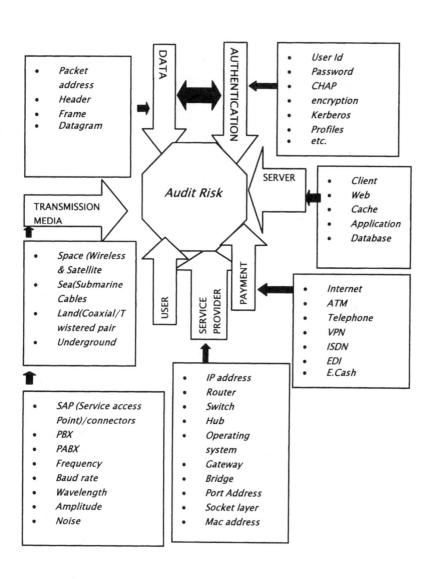

Figure 8

(RISG) Risk Identification Solution Grid Level 6

	Z1	Z2	Z3	Z4	Z5	Z6	Z7
Z1	Skill	Satellite	Gateway	Repeater	Frame	Router	Client Server
Z2	Location	VPN	Terminator	Socket layer	Connectors	Frequency	SAP (Service Access Provider)
Z3	Hub	EDI	E-Chip	Password	Cable/Wire	Cache Server	Port address
Z4	Switch	E-cash	OSS	Cyphertext	Profile	Dbase Server	MAC address
Z5	Baudrate	ATM	VPN	PBX	Application	Web Server	Datagram
Z6	Bandwith	Packet address	Earth station	SAP	Amplitude	ISP	Protocol
Z7	IP-Address	Router	Wavelength	USER ID/PIN	Sec. Provider	Noise	Circuit

SOLUTIONS

5.4 Synchronising E-Security Methodology

The ideas central to Synchronising E-security Methodology are based on risk identification, extraction, integration, audit and a risk identification solution grid derived from risk access spots on network and operating system platforms. Figures 3 to 8 are pictorial and graphical representations of the ideas presented in this text.

This section introduces a number of concepts that explains the techniques adopted by the methodology. The following are concepts central to the methodology: (RAS) Risk Access Spots introduced as a footnote in section 5.2, (RIG) Risk Identification Grid, (RISG) Risk Identification Solutions Grid and (Z) Zones.

5.4.1 (RAS) Risk Access Spots

RAS are areas of risk that could be perceived, actual or emerge as a hoax and could be vulnerable to threat or attack. Identifying RAS is the first level of this methodology. RAS are not permanent, although certain areas could be recommended as risk prone than other areas. RAS are dynamic and might not necessarily follow any particular pattern. The identification of RAS should be followed by risk extraction. Extracting the risk and documenting the risk is essential to providing solutions. The risk extracts are documented using the (RIG) Risk Identification Grid in figure 5.

5.4.2 (RIG) Risk Identification Grid

RIG is a two-dimensional array grid comprising RAS and (Z) Zones. The Zones are demarcated areas where risk could be perceived or emerge. Synchronising E-Security methodology proposes seven Zones as hypothetical risk regions. The proposition is based on the notion that RAS emerge at different levels of network and operating systems, which support international, national, city, town, company or an organisation's electronic transactions. The risk access spots identified on RIG is integrated. The purpose of the integration is to determine common and non-common risk amongst the seven Zones in the RIG which represent network and operating system platforms in any geographical region. (See figure 6). The process of risk integration is followed by a risk audit, which creates a synthesis of perceived and actual risk (See figure 7). Solutions are then provided for the actual risk whiles contingencies are put in place to monitor the perceived risk using the RISG. An expert or the proposed simulator in this text could be consulted to deal with the RAS documented in the RIG. The concepts that drive Synchronising E-Security Methodology have been modelled using (SSTM) Service Server Transmission Model in figure 3, 4, 6 and 7 of section 5.3.

5.5 Discussions on SSTM and RAS

This section is an introduction to critical risk access spots of the SSTM. The set of SSTM form the central ideas of the methodology. The main components of the SSTM are the following: Transmission Media; Service Provider; Server; Payment; Authentication; Data; User.

5.5.1 Transmission Media

The main RAS identified from Transmission media are (SAP) Service Access Points or Connectors, Terminators, (PBX) Private Branch Exchanges, (PABX) Public Automatic Branch Exchanges, the Electromagnetic spectrum comprising Frequency, Wavelength, Amplitude, Baud rate, Base band and Noise and Wired media (twisted pair, coaxial cable, fibre optic etc).

5.5.1.1 (SAP) Service Access Point

A SAP is a point of interconnection where two or more (n) number of services exchange information on a computer network in the form of packets[2], digital or analogue signals. This information could be passed from a switch, connector or port of a (LAN) local area network to a (WAN) wide area network via a router (*see section 5.5.2 for detail descriptions*). The poor termination of these ports and connectors could result in RAS. Services are enabled by protocols[3], which are either connection, or connectionless oriented. Examples of such protocols are (TCP) Transmission Control Protocol and (UDP) User Datagram Protocol. Services could also be passed through an electromagnetic spectrum. Although most authors do not classify electromagnetic spectrum as a SAP, the author believes that since services could be provided using wireless media, it will be appropriate to consider that as a SAP. A similar notion has

---

[2] Electronic block of data that shows it source and destination via an address.

[3] Set of guidelines that govern the format of communication

been introduced by Deutsche Telecom known as *"Hotspots"*[4] .The application of security threats such as traffic analysis, brute force and sniffing of packet addresses make SAP to become RAS. Techniques such as traffic analysis and packet sniffing jeopardise the confidentiality of information across the network. In chapter 1 we discussed authentication as a means of ensuring integrity, the acquisition of confidential information could be used as means of violating the integrity of information used for electronic transactions in banking environments.

5.5.1.2 (ES) Electromagnetic Spectrum and RAS

Section 5.5.1.1 introduced electromagnetic spectrum as a RAS in wireless communication. Although there are several definitions given to the electromagnetic spectrum (see Dean 2003), this text defines it as a vacuum or empty space where light or sound waves could travel. Electromagnetic spectrum comprises waves. A wave is a form of signal that propagates itself via electrons which are electrically charged. *(It is not the scope of this book to cover electrons)*. Although a signal in an electromagnetic spectrum is not physical, an example of a wave could be represented by dropping a stone in a bowl of water. The ripples that appear as a result of the immersion are examples of waves *(Sea Waves)*. Concepts such as bandwidth, wavelength, frequency, amplitude and noise within the electromagnetic spectrum could serve as risk access spots.

Bandwidth of a transmission refers to the range of frequencies that could be transmitted through a communication channel. An example is the bandwidth allocated to national and international security services. Frequencies unknown, foreign or illegal could be transmitted deliberately or accidentally through these allocated bandwidths. Intruders could use techniques and methods such as signal propagation from transistors to intercept, reduce or amplify messages within these frequencies. This might result in noise or attenuation[5]. This could be interpreted as intrusion or interference. The "Hotspots" of such signal and service exchange points within wireless data transmission environments could be vulnerable to attack.

Frequency refers to the number of transmission cycles in a wave. The nature of frequencies could vary depending of the intensity of the signal

---

[4] Access Points within wireless Networks

[5] The reduction of the power or intensity of a transmitted signal

80

transmitted. For instance the human voice could generate a frequency range different from sound emissions from the horn of a train.

Amplitude refers to the highest point a signal could travel or propagate itself from source to destination of transmission.

Figure 9 - Electromagnetic Spectrum

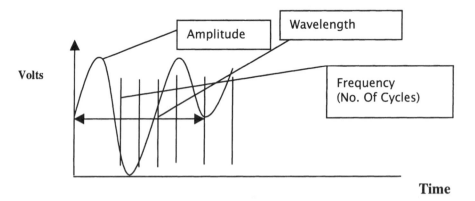

5.5.2 Service Provider

Chapters 3 and 4 discussed issues related to ISPs across the globe. Empirical analysis of studies conducted showed that ISPs globally did not operate on similar standards and policies, although there were e-trade and e-commerce activities in both developing and advanced economies. This section examines addressing systems of ISPs by assessing risk spots of IP, PORT "Number" and MAC addresses.

5.5.2.1 IP Address

IP (Internet Protocol) address comprises a network number and PC or host number allocated internally or externally. The internal allocation of IP address is known as a private unofficial IP address. This consists of a network and a host number. Officially, network numbers are allocated by a non-profit making organisation known as *(ICANN) Internet Corporation for Assigned Names and Numbers.* The rationale behind such a de facto standard is to avoid confusion on the Internet. IP addresses represent the source and destination of packet information. The object of an IP address is primarily to enable routing of information across the Internet. Every network linked or interfaced to the Internet via a router has an IP address.

In other words a router has IP information regarding all networks linked to itself. (See figure 10).

IP address consists of 32 bits organised in four octets[6]. These bits are converted or translated to decimal numbers that could be read by non-technical persons. For instance an IP address in the form 11000000.10010001.00000001.00000001 could be converted to decimal as 192.145.1.1. An IP address in a decimal form 177.132.1.1 is also represented in binary as 10110001.10000101.00000001.00000001. This is achieved by converting base 10 numbers to base 2 and vice versa. Adopting masquerading techniques could be a means of creating deception among IP addresses. Although standard security systems mask IP addresses, the masks could sometimes be unveiled using virus attacks or brute force. Poor masking of IP addresses could result in RAS. IP numbers stored on routing tables of a router could be a valuable source of information to hackers and intruders.

Figure 10 - Internetworking of N1 (Network1) & N2 (Network2) via a Router

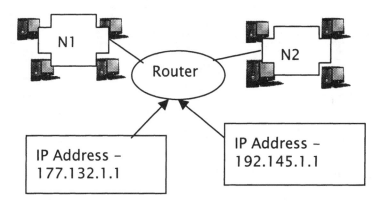

The application of IPv6 in mobile environments using mobile devices brings a number of unanswered questions to mind. Questions relating to security intelligence and robustness provided by foreign and local agents that secure access points of portable mobile devices serve as RAS. For instance how does the home agent determine and verify the authenticity of

---

[6] Block of eight bits

82

a foreign agent? What protocol is used to ensure trust and integrity? These are risk-associated problems that have not been addresses satisfactorily.

5.5.2.2 PORT AND PORT NUMBER

Section 5.5.1.1 discussed SAP highlighting ports and connectors as entry points to computer networks. A port is a point of connection attached to an electronic device. It might not necessarily be a computer. It could however form an integral part of a computer system. This could range from printers, scanners, cameras, hubs, switches, (NICs) Network Interface Cards, mobile phones etc. Trojans and sniffing software could be used to listen or analyse PORT numbers. Figure 11 shows a list of port numbers usually used by Trojans and sniffing software to create deception and subsequently obtain information regarding the sources and destination of data across networks.

Figure 11 - Trojans and Port numbers

TROJAN	PORT NUMBER
Devil	65000
Deep Throat	UDP 2140 and 3150
Girl Friend	TCP 21544
Evil FTP	23456
Gate Crasher	6969
Remote Grab	7000
Temptation	53001
Angel	4590
Mirage	7789

Source: Dayspring Ltd and NOBA research.

Methods of dealing with, and assessing the state of ports vary. Intrusion detection systems or utility managers could be used to examine the state of ports on a network. More sophisticated methods using intelligent agents could also be adopted. It is not the subject of this book to discuss such methods. Figure 12 lists common default Port numbers active on most networks including the Internet.

Figure 12 - Default Port numbers

Port Number	Description
80	Web server Port(IP address)
110	Pop server Port(mail services)
137, 138,139	NetBIOS/TCP/IP Port
25	SMTP Server(works in conjunction with Port 80) mail services
23	Telnet Server
443	Secure Socket Layer server Port
21	FTP Server
1352	Lotus notes RPC Port
1393	Network Log Server

Source: Dayspring Ltd & NOBA Research

The above port numbers could serve as entry points for intruders and hackers if not managed effectively. For instance in figure 11, I highlighted port numbers adopted by Trojans to eavesdrop information transmitted via ports that could serve as a means of violating security discussed in section 5.5.2.2. A port number selected randomly between 1024 and 65535 will work as long as the number is not in use.

5.5.2.3 MAC ADDRESS

MAC is referred to as *Medium Access Control*. The purpose of MAC is basically to identify every physical device on a computer network and establish communication amongst these devices. The physical device in this context refers to the (NIC) Network Interface Card. The address given to the NIC is the MAC address. A typical MAC address will be for instance 0000C0FBB1A4 or 0000C0F958A3.They are referred to in certain literature as LAN, NODE, Adapter, Ethernet or Physical addresses. It is however referred to in this text as MAC address for the sake of consistency. MAC addresses serve as a tool in gaining unauthorised access unto networks. Any information that helps to identify and locate Network Interface Cards such as a MAC address could be detrimental to the security of networks.

5.5.2.3 SERVER

A *Server* is a program resident on a computer that responds to a request made by a user via another program known as a *Client* on any electronic network, although it is generally referred as a computer network. Several connotations and definitions given to a Server refer to it, as a computer that replies to request made by users. The author believes that such a definition restricts the application of Servers. The argument put forward here is based on the notion that Servers that respond to Client requests might not necessarily reside on computers. Any electronic device capable of responding to request from Clients regardless of geographical location might be classified as a Server as a matter of principle. Similarly computer programs making request for services on Servers might not be also made from a computer. The deployment device or hardware and the program that responds to such services as defined earlier could also be represented as a Server. The entry point of a Server is via the port number allocated to the Server (See examples in figure 12). The Client should also know the port number allocated to the Server in order to gain entry to the Server. Intruders and hackers could use remote invocations and method calls to access the resources placed on a Server. IP address and Port number could be combined to form a Socket. A Socket derives it's address from an IP address and a Port number.

5.6 Authentication

Chapter 1 provided an overview of the authentication process in Telebanking. This section highlights aspects of authentication, which the author suggests as critical in the Telebanking process. These are User Profiles and Cyphertext *(Encrypted message)*.

5.6.1 User Profile

Chapter 1 discussed User Profiling as a method of capturing the attributes of the User of a Telebanking system. Profiling the user is important because it allows service providers to detect unusual behaviour of users. Building the necessary intelligence to provide information on *geographical locations* of users instantly is an effective method of identifying RAS in specific geographical locations. Patterns and frequency of user system interaction could be a valuable source of information.

5.6.2 Cyphertext

A Cyphertext is an encrypted message. Techniques such as crypt-analysis and pattern analysis are the most common methods used in decrypting a Cyphertext. Although the primary objective of encrypting a message is to ensure confidentiality, this objective is loosely achieved in most cases. It is argued here that encryption ensures integrity rather than confidentiality. The application of techniques such as crypt-analysis could permit eavesdropping (*See Smart 2003*) for detail information on Cryptography.
Reasons why these systems fail were discussed in section 1.6.1.1 and 1.6.1.2. The Cyphertext is not usually vulnerable to attack. It is rather the paths, nodes and links via which the Cyphertext travel, become access of attack. In section 5.5.2.2 there were discussions on Ports and Port numbers. Ports serve as entry points for Cyphertexts. The Ports that link different nodes and host in a network environment becomes a RAS that banks should provide utmost protection against.

5.7 Forensics and Evidence Collection

Figure 13 is a summary of all the critical RAS speculated by the author using evidence collection in computer forensics. The importance of evidence collection is to "flag" RAS in a pre and post violation attack.

Figure 13: Evidence Collection of RAS

IP address	Port Number	MAC address	Server (Socket Address)
User Profile		Cyphertext	
Location	Attributes		
Bandwidth	Frequency	Amplitude	Wavelength
Connectors	Terminators	Transceivers	Receivers

5.7.1 Evidence collection via principle of negotiation

In this section I introduce the principle of negotiation as a method of evidence collection. RAS provides a basis for evidence collection in pre and post security violations. The technique proposed for obtaining such evidence is termed in this text as *principle of negotiation via RAS.*

5.7.2 Principle of Negotiation by RAS

The principle states that in order to secure RAS, there should be a negotiation between defence and attack. The objective of the negotiation is to identify actual and perceived risk and act upon them accordingly. This is achieved via implementing a program embedded with this principle. Level 5 of the methodology formulates the solution to this problem. It is stipulated here that the principle will be used in conjunction with existing security layers, such as firewalls, SET (Secure Electronic Transaction), and SSL (Secure Socket Layer). A detail description of this principle has been outlined as part of future work.

5.8 Summary of Chapter 5

Chapter 5 consolidated the ideas discussed in this book by the application of Synchronising E-Security Methodology, which is part of the proposed toolkit for Synchronising E-Security Methods. The (SSTM) Service and Server Transmission Models were introduced as techniques for implementing the Methodology. (RAS) Risk Access Spots of the (RIG) Risk Integration Grid and the (RISG) Risk Integration and Solutions Grid formed integral parts of the Methodology. Evidence collection via RAS using the principle of negotiation was proposed as a technique for monitoring pre and post security violations.

5.9 CONCLUSIONS

The study provided an insight into technologies that supported electronic transactions in international banking. Issues regarding the impact of security on the end user were examined and assessed. It was found that authentication methods formed the critical phase of any security system, upholding main goals of security, thus integrity, availability and confidentiality. The investigations depicted that it was possible to violate the confidentiality of any financial transaction if the identification and verification processes within authentication were not met with the appropriate measures. The absence of such measures makes information regarding a particular transaction available to unscrupulous persons. This could result in a breach of confidentiality which is a key goal in security.

Technical and non technical manpower that supported e-security were highlighted. The human ware was seen to be an important and critical aspect of security in information systems. The manpower in most organisations perceived risk differently due to culture and the environment where these systems were implemented. It was learnt that judgements made on the importance of laid down procedures for ensuring risk prevention were dependent on individuals within organisations. There were also disparities in skills possessed by the manpower of developing and advanced economies. Poor implementation and management processes caused security failure.

Economics of security was also discussed with emphasis on equilibrium of economies, and how economies affected risk and fraud. The studies indicated that there was a gap in risk mitigating and prevention technologies between developing and advanced economies.

There was an examination of communications infrastructure across the globe. Emphasis was placed on the services provided by ISPs. Weaknesses in security that existed in the framework of electronic fund transfer, Internet and Telephone banking were highlighted as weaknesses that could be exploited by electronic criminals. The lack of a holistic approach to authentication highlighted the need for improvements via synchronisation. It was discussed that the rules that constituted the design of security policies and algorithms did not integrate risk factors that evolved from operating systems platforms of developing economies. It was also discussed that e-trade was on the ascendancy in both developing and advanced economies although there were instances of Dot Com failures. Synchronisation of e-security methods was vital in loosening the chains of e-trade regulations in advanced economies. It was also seen as a means of making e-trade friendlier to developing economies. The human ware for both technical and non-technical manpower left much to be desired in both developing and advanced economies. The assessment also revealed that there was an escalation of risk.

The ideas discussed in this book are based on the application of Synchronising E-Security Methodology, an integral part of the proposed toolkit for Synchronising E-Security Methods. The (SSTM) Service Server Transmission Models were introduced as techniques for implementing the

Methodology. (RAS) Risk Access Spots of the (RIG) Risk Integration Grid and the (RISG) Risk Integration and Solutions Grid formed integral parts of the Methodology. Evidence collection via RAS using the principle of negotiation has been proposed as a technique for monitoring pre and post security violations. In a nutshell the evidences from the empirical studies drives home a number of points that should be further examined and verified.

5.9.1 Future Developments

Models of the proposed methodology derived from guidelines will be developed into a risk assessment software simulator as a complete toolkit for synchronising-e security methods in the near future.

REFERENCES/BIBLIOGRAPHY

Adams, J.(1999). The management of risk and uncertainty. Policy analysis no. 335[cultural filters of risk]

Akerlofi, G.A (1970). "The market for lemons; Quality uncertainty and market mechanism " Quarterly journal of economics volume 84.

Albright, B (1999) Wireless makes bigger waves, Automatic I.D. News(USA) 15 (13) . 16 - 19

Anderson J. (1973). Computer security Technology planning study; ESD-TR-T3-51, US Air force electronic systems division..

Anderson R.J. (2001). Security Engineering. A guide to building dependable distributed systems; Wiley. ISBN 0-471-38922-6

Anderson R.J. (1994). "Why cryptosystems fail" in communications of the ACM vol. 37 no. 11. pp 32-40.

Anderson. R.J (1992). A second generation Electronic Wallet. Computer Security. Springer LNCS.

Bloom et al. (1999). " copy protection for DVD video", in proceedings of the IEEE volume 87 no. 7. pp 1267 – 1276.

Burrows(1992). A logic Authentication. SRC Research Report 39

Campbell et al.(1997) IMIS journal December 1997. The Global electronic bazaar. 24

Campbell, Calvert, Boswell. Cisco Learning Institute (2003) Security + guide to network security fundamentals. Thomson course technology.

Capers Jones (1997). "The Year 2000 Problem: International Strategies and solutions for the Fortune 100", Thomson Computer Press.

Central Intelligence Agency (2002). World Fact Book

Com(2001). European Union., Network and information security. Proposal for an European Policy Approach; 298 final.

Collins(1992). Bank worker guilty of ATM fraud. Sunday Times

Dean Tamara(2003). Guide to Telecommunication Technology

Delloite and Touche e-Commerce Security: A global status report.

Ellof M.M. & Solms von S.H.(2002)698-709, Information Security Management: An approach to combine process certfication and product evaluation, computers & security.

Evans P. B.and Wurster S. Thomas(1997). September-October. 76 Havard Business Review. Retail banks will not become obsolete, but their current definition will.

FBI(2002). Annual FBI Surveys

Fourouzan B.A (2001). Data Communication and Networks. McGrawHill

Glasson et al. Information Systems and technology in the international office of the future. Chapman & Hall. 30,31,34

Gonzi Lawrence.(2001), Social Policy MinisterOn banking, unions and industrial relations, The Malta financial & business times.

Hudson.,Caudle.,Cannon(2003). CCNA Guide to Cisco Networking. Thomson

Ian,. B et al. (2002). Electronic commerce. Who carries the risks of fraud ? Journal of Information, Law and Technology.

ILO (International Labour Organisation)., ICT and Decent Work: Finding Solutons in the Information Society.

InfoServe(2000). World Bank report on Y2K initiative. *Extracts from news release No. 99/2078/s.*

Kahin and Varian(2000).internet publishing and beyond. The economics of Digital information and Intellectual Property. MIT Press.

Leon-Garcia.,Widjaja (2000). Communication Networks: Fundamentals Concepts and Key Architectures. McGraw-Hill Series in Computer Science

Jones Rob (1997). July Business and Technology Journal. Net can't catch Cyber criminals.

Keen. P.,Mackintosh.R (2001).The Freedom Economy. Gaining the M-commerce Edge in the Era of the Wireless Internet. ISBN: 0-07-213367-8. McGrawHill.

Kurose and Ross(2003). Computer Networking: A Top-Down Approach Featuring the Internet. Pearson Education

Lloyd W. F (1833). Two lectures on the checks to population. Oxford University Press.

Mestchian,.P (2003). Risk Business. The Economist June 7th - 13th.

NAP(1990),. Computers at risk. Safe computing in the information age. "Why the security market has not worked well, pp. 143 -178.
National Institute of standards and Technology. Technology Administration. U.S. Dept of commerce. 800-30. A US government guide

Odlyzko A(2001). Economics, Psychology and Sociology of security. Digital Technology Centre, University of Minnesota, 499 Walter Library, 117

Panko.R.R. Enduser Computing(Management Application & Technology). John Wiler & Sons. 34,35,36

Pleasant st. SE . Minneapolis, MN 55455, USA.

Rigby R.(1997). Management Today. Mondex's master card.

Shapiro, C., Varian H (1998). 'Information Rules', Havard Business School Press (1998). ISBN 0-87584-863-X.

Smart Nigel (2003). Cryptography: An introduction. McGraw-Hill

Spar D.and Bussgang J. J.(1996)May-June. Havard Business Review. Means of Exchange and Security enforcement.129-131, 131-132

Tanenbaum.,A.S. (2003). Computer Networks. Pearson

Townsend Kevin(1997). IMIS journal. July 1997. 22, 23

Varian H.(2000). Managing on-line security risks. New York Times.
An analysis of cash machines fraud.

Vulkan., N. (2003). The Economics of E-commerce. A strategic guide to understanding and designing the online market place. ISBN: 0-691-08906-X. Princeton University Press.

Viscount Chelmsford(1998) March.8,9. Institute for the management of information systems(IMIS) journal. Electronic commerce reality or Myth.

Williams, G. & Avudzivi P.V.(2002). A retrospective view on information security management. The impact of tele-banking on the end-user. Proceedings of the 2nd Hawaii international conference on business.

Williams, G & Avudzivi P.V.(2003). Risk assessment methods for technologies that support e-commerce transactions in developing economies (A study in Ghana). Proceedings of the 3rd Hawaii international conference on business.

Williams, G(2003). A dive into policies and international laws that create security gaps in global electronic transactions among developing economies. Proceedings of the 3rd Hawaii international conference on business.

Williams, G & Oynango E.K (2003) The impact of electronic commerce on small businesses in UK economy. Proceedings of the 3rd Hawaii international conference on business.

Yen D.C, Kane.,J(2001). Breaking the barriers of connectivity: analysis of the Wireless LAN. Elseiver., Computer Standards and Interfaces.
http://www.isaca.org/standard/procedure1.pdf
http://www.forrester.com

GLOSSARY OF TERMS

(FO) Fiber-optic cable - A multichannel communications cable using a thread of optical glass fibers as a transmission medium in which the signal (voice, video, etc.) is in the form of a coded pulse of light.

Intelsat - International Telecommunications Satellite Organization (Washington, DC).

Telephone/Landline - Communication wire or cable of any sort that is installed on poles or buried in the ground.

(MRRL) Microwave radio relay - Transmission of long distance telephone calls and television programs by highly directional radio microwaves that are received and sent on from one booster station to another on an optical path.

Satellite communication system (INTELSAT) - a communication system consisting of two or more earth stations and at least one satellite that provide long distance transmission of voice, data, and television; the system usually serves as a trunk connection between telephone exchanges; if the earth stations are in the same country, it is a domestic system.

(SES) Satellite earth station - a communications facility with a microwave radio transmitting and receiving antenna and required receiving and transmitting equipment for communicating with satellites.

(SC) Submarine cable - A cable designed for service under water.

(WLL) Wireless Local Loop

(CC) Coaxial Cable

(MC) Mobile Cellular

(DMRR) Digital Microwave Radio Relay

(OECD) Organisation for economic cooperation and development

Appendix 1

- A test to determine a company's participation or adoption of any national or international security policy and standard and the type of standard adopted if there was any.
- A test on estimated investment in security risk prevention technology?

The estimation was based on the following ranges.
- None
- - $1000
- 1000 - $5000
- 5000- $10,000
- above $10,000

- A test on estimated investment in security risk assessment exercises?
  The estimation was based on the following ranges.
- None
- - $1000
- 1000 - $5000
- 5000- $10,000
- above $10,000

- A test on risk assessment methods used or adopted by companies.
- A test on frequency of risk assessment exercises?
- A test of security expertise in the following areas

| LINUX/UNIX |
| NOVELL NETWARE |
| WINDOWS |
| CISCO Technology |

- A test on servers used by the ISPs. Examples:

Server vendor is Microsoft and server type is Microsoft-IIS
Server vendor is Apache and server type is Apache-SSL

- An assessment of security areas vulnerable to attack

INDEX

A

Africa, 23, 24, 44, 46, 48, 51, 52, 62, 64
Amplitude, 80, 83, 85, 87, 93
ASIA, 62, 64
Assessment, 41, 47, 48, 58
ATM, 1, 80, 83, 97
Australia, 47
Authentication, 7, 8, 9, 19, 85, 91, 97

B

Bandwagon, 37, 49, 57, 74
Banking, 38, 60, 67
Baud rate, 85
Biometrics, 8, 16

C

Case study, 39
CHAP, 8, 16, 17
CIA, 58, 63
CISCO, 101
Coaxial, 58, 100
Communications, 62
Confidentiality, 54
Cryptography, 92, 99
Cyphertext, 80, 83, 92, 93

D

Datagram, 80, 83, 86

E

Economic, 60
Economics, 94, 98, 99
Economy, 98
EDI, 1, 80, 83
electronic, 1, 2, 3, 5, 6, 7, 8, 9, 11, 13,
    16, 19, 23, 34, 35, 36, 37, 50, 51, 54,
    67, 68, 69, 70, 72, 84, 86, 89, 91, 94,
    95, 96, 97, 99
Electronic Wallet, 5, 97
Empirical, 56, 87
End-user, 1, 2, 3, 4, 22

e-security, 21, 26, 39, 41, 54, 67, 69, 70,
    71, 72, 74, 94, 95
e-trading, 69, 70
Europe, 53

F

Fibre Optic, 59
Frame, 80, 83
fraud, 3, 4, 5, 10, 23, 35, 54, 94, 97, 98,
    99
Frequency, 15, 80, 83, 85, 87, 93

G

Gateway, 80, 83
guidelines, 72, 74, 86, 96

H

Hardware, 30, 38, 41
holistic, 36, 37, 68, 70, 72, 95
HSA, 11
Human, 8, 9, 11, 12

I

Infrastructure, 61, 62
Integrity, 54
International, 1, 33, 36, 50, 59, 97, 98,
    100
Internet, 1, 2, 3, 4, 6, 7, 9, 10, 12, 13, 15,
    18, 19, 23, 51, 52, 58, 60, 62, 63, 67,
    68, 69, 70, 88, 90, 95, 98
ISMS, 28, 30, 54
ITSEC, 53

J

JAD, 36

K

Kerberos, 9, 16, 17, 18, 19

M

MAC, 80, 83, 87, 90, 93